Intuitive Self Care

Creating An Owner's Manual For Self

MONICA HURT MSSW, LMFT

Edited by: Brenda "Scout" Watkins

This book is dedicated to Thomas, who helps me heal daily by showing me love I never imagined possible. To Elliott & Cooper, you are my reasons for everything, you have been the motivation for this journey because I wanted more for you both. To Kurt, Julia, & Ian, thank you for loving us and sharing your Dad. To my parents, I wouldn't have made it without your help. I love and appreciate you all.

Table of Contents

Introduction

"The Journey of a thousand miles begins with one step."

— Lao Tzu

This is, without a doubt, my favorite quote. It had a profound impact on me and how I now view life. The thing about quotes is that you have to be in the right place and time for them to exert influence. In other words, had I not been ready, it would have been just another cool saying that I read. Thankfully, that was not the case.

So, where was I when I read this important message? I was sitting in my home office fumbling with schoolwork or being upset with life, maybe trying to figure out why I was so depressed, or how the hell I'd been in a bad relationship for so long. You know, the regular, woe is me crap, when we are anything but happy with our lives. Whatever it was, I read the quote, and it hit me like a ton of bricks.

To be honest, I needed something to speak to me because I had spent years trying to figure out who I was, how to be who I wanted to be, and how not to just exist in the chaos that was my life. I was officially stuck, but after years of living in Stuckville, I felt hopeful.

Now, as with most anything else in my life, I will get an idea or thought in my head, and I have to examine it every way I possibly can until I decide how I can move forward. This motivation was no different, although I wish I could say I jumped into action and made the life I wanted immediately, the truth is it took me a minute. But I was motivated, and once that happens, I will always find a way.

Fast forward a couple of years, and I am sitting in a Marriage & Family Therapist (MFT) conference. I had decided that I could help others by becoming a psychotherapist because I had been through so much crap. You know, a been there, done that, sort of thing. Plus, I thought maybe I could help myself, my partner, my family, and possibly my friends, with all the crazy that we had been through.

There I was waiting to attend a lecture with Dr. John Lentz. If I'm being honest, I probably wasn't thrilled to be at the conference. I had two babies at home and a partner who was struggling with mental illness. However, it was a requirement, and I wanted to see what his hypnotherapy lecture was all about. I had heard about Dr. Lentz and his work in hypnotherapy. His reputation was of an eclectic spirit, little did I know he was considered a rock star in the MFT community. Either way, I was curious.

As I walked into the room, I was immediately struck by the energy. It felt different from the stuffy lectures I had seen the day before. I took notice at the slide that was on the whiteboard and thought, oh yeah, this is what I'm talking about. It was a picture of Dr. Lentz and his wife on the top of a mountain with clouds beneath them. They looked so happy, and at peace, it was like something out of a magazine. It was certainly not something I had ever seen any of my friends or family bring home from their vacations. Needless to say, I was intrigued and a little sad. The picture was of a life I only dreamed of, especially given my current situation. Hell, buying diapers was a struggle, I'd have to win the lottery to be able to do something like that. Nonetheless, I wanted to know what it felt like to be above the clouds, but also to exude joy from head to toe. Dr. Lentz had gotten there; maybe I should listen up.

As I made my way toward the front of the room, I noticed Dr. Lentz and his kind smile. He had a calmness about him that made me uneasy at first, mostly because I had never encountered a species like that before. How does one emit so much calm and be at such peace without even opening their mouth? Why was his energy so palpable? I needed to know more, so I sat front and center.

As the lecture began, I felt my shoulders relax, and my breathing start to slow. Wait a minute, what the hell is going on here? Is this man hypnotizing me? What I learned he was doing was changing my trance or state of mind. Sadly, I had never experienced anything like that before, and honestly never even thought it was possible. I mean, I lived in chaos for most of my life, it never occurred to me that there was any other way to live. I never imagined that you could slow things down and feel different, connect with self, and be present. I had never slowed down to be present in life. I was only existing, getting from moment to moment, thankful to get through the minutes, only to fall into my bed every night so I could begin planning the next day. I was merely surviving.

Once I realized what was happening, I think I cried. It was as if the Universe was giving me what I needed, even though I didn't know I needed it. John Lentz stood there in the sunlight, that February day and orchestrated something magical for me, he revealed a path, and it would be up to me to follow the road. I always tell people about meeting John and how I wished I could put him in my pocket. He helped me begin my journey into mindfulness, self-care, self-awareness, being present, and living in joy.

Once again, I wish I could say I immediately went home and began a new life, being present, and escaping the chaos. I am part sloth and do nothing quickly. The truth is it took a hot minute, but damn if I didn't find my way. I will always be grateful for Dr. Lentz. Without his lecture that day, I'm not sure how well I would have done, or if I would have survived.

Why write a book about self-care? Well, it turns out that self-care is what I had always left out. I never knew what it was, nor did I understand the power of it. Most importantly, I didn't know how to do it moment by moment in an effort to self-regulate. What Dr. Lentz showed me was just a tiny snippet into the world of being at peace. I think most people aren't taught to be mindful or learn how to deal with emotions, let alone be able to take care of themselves during times of stress, emotional pain, depression, anxiety, or trauma. I can say with confidence that given my life experiences, and over ten years of doing psychotherapy, I know people are not coping well with emotions. Therefore, I wanted to break it down and make it an easy path for anyone. Life doesn't have to be as hard as we make it, especially if we are given the proper tools to navigate the way.

My goal is to help you find your way through the journey of life with ease and calm. Life throws things at us that we do not know how to deal with. We aren't given an owner's manual, but we can create one for ourselves if we do the work and continue doing so for the rest of our lives. What exactly is Intuitive Self Care (ISC) and how can it help you? Self-care is about knowing who you are and what you need to function on an optimal level. It's about knowing how you best operate while living life in a mindful way.

We often forget about ourselves because we are so busy doing, going, and taking care of others that we forget about self, or just don't have anything left to give. This causes people to be overwhelmed and stressed out. These two things, in particular, lead to negative self-talk, low self-esteem, negative coping skills, and worsened physical and mental health issues. I see how this new way of life is wreaking havoc on so many of us. I believe it is avoidable, but we have to learn to operate differently and take care of ourselves proactively.

In my practice, I see patients that suffer from various traumas and disorders like depression, anxiety, OCD, PTSD, and bipolar disorder. As a Marriage & Family Therapist, and AASECT trained Sex Therapist, I work with individuals, couples, and entire families dealing with everything from infidelity to raising kids and divorce. I also work with LGBTQA+ folks, people in non-monogamous relationships, and those practicing consensual BDSM activities. I call it, Traditional to Fringe. The thing that all these peeps have in common is that they are stuck for some reason and they need my help to figure out how to get unstuck.

If you want to navigate life in a mindful state, and you want to stop getting stuck on your old crap, this book is for you. I can help you figure out your baggage, or what I call Knowns. These are life experiences that have created narratives, often applying emphasis on the negative, that becomes a part of who we are, marking turning points, limiting our options, and possibly changing our life direction. Frequently, Knowns will be identified as traumas that have shaped you, as well as helped create a belief system about yourself, others, and the world around you. Knowns can be influenced by our ideas and belief systems. False or limiting beliefs may have been damaging, often formulated throughout your life and changed how you live.

Once we have determined the Knowns, we begin understanding the Root Causes. The roots are the pathways by which these traumas, experiences, tendencies, beliefs, and quirks were created. After the roots are determined, we move on to mindfulness. Mindfulness gives us the space to make better, more informed decisions by teaching us to evaluate our environment and self. Utilizing mindfulness allows us to recognize how the Knowns and roots affect us on a daily basis. Next, we work on Embracing Vulnerability. Being vulnerable allows us to let people in and helps push us toward being more authentic. All of these tools combine to create a better understanding of self and make ISC an incredible way of navigating through life while not allowing your crap to hold you back.

Once we grasp the tools for ISC, we begin working on our self-care list. Creating a comprehensive self-care list is going to be ever-changing, but something you will utilize for your entire life. After you become versed in using your self-care list, we will then move on to understanding your Energy Signature. An energy signature is how you present yourself to the world and influence how people perceive you, which is an essential concept because we need to be completely aware of ourselves.

Next, we progress toward learning who we want to be. This is an important question and one I think we should all be asking ourselves on the regular. That is one of the things I encourage people to do when they run into situations that are challenging. Ask yourself, who do I want to be in this situation? This concept is rooted in mindfulness and expands the practice of ISC even further.

Finally, we put it all together and create an Owner's Manual for Self. Throughout the book, you will see questions that will help prompt you to make notes to help develop your personal owner's manual. This is an exciting concept because we can then truly navigate life in a way that allows us to heal from what has caused us harm. We can create the life we desire because we are no longer stuck repeating the same cycles expecting different outcomes. We become self-actualized, which is when we truly understand ourselves and how we operate. We become intuitive about the entire process and it becomes how we operate daily without giving it a thought. We ultimately create a navigation system for happiness, calm, and peace within ourselves.

I hope that becoming intuitive about self allows you to become the calm, positive, happy person we all want to be. You will learn how you became you and, in turn, create the you, you've always wanted to be. I can't promise it will be easy, because you come to grips with some truths that may not be so wonderful. However, you will see those things differently, and they will no longer have the same power over you that they once had. Instead of just trying to let them go, we will learn to heal and be able to move forward. I always say to my peeps, you can't just forget about the things that made you who you are today, but you can decide if it's something that's useful. You can determine if it still fits in your life, you can decide if it's who you want to be. Once you have accomplished these things, you get to maneuver your life in a way that your old crap doesn't have power over you anymore. Through self-care, you learn about what you need, when, why, and how to get it.

I am happy to say that I have become what Dr. John Lentz modeled for me. I am calm. I am happy, and I know how to do self-care so that I never return to that place of chaos. I found my way, and I invite you to dare go on this life-changing journey for yourself.

What Is Intuitive Self Care?

"Self-care has become a new priority – the revelation that it's perfectly permissible to listen to your body and do what it needs."

— Frances Ryan

Self-care and mindfulness saved my life. Yes, I am aware of how dramatic it sounds, but it's true. I was absolutely miserable emotionally and physically. Remarkably, if you weren't in my inner circle, you wouldn't have known how awful things were. I kept it hidden like it was a state secret. Meanwhile, at work, I was smiling like I was getting paid extra. My ability to hide my reality was rather impressive to the untrained eye. Sadly, I was in an abusive marriage, depressed, and had an undiagnosed autoimmune disorder that was exacerbated by all the stress in my life. If you'd met me back in the day, you probably wouldn't have recognized me. I looked different; I was heavier, my skin was a wreck, I didn't smile, and had perpetual resting bitch face. Outside of work, I was so negative, and in such physical pain, that I looked the epitome of misery. Looking back, I only survived because I loved my kids so much that I knew I had to make changes, or this would be their fate as well. There were times

I felt incredibly conflicted because I knew what I was saying didn't match what I was doing. No words can describe how awful that felt.

Beyond my children bringing me happiness, I was engrossed in being a helper to my patients. I so enjoyed helping others, even though I couldn't help myself, or so I thought. I was all in with my patients, assisting other people in changing came naturally to me; it wasn't as easy to see that I was capable of doing the same for myself. Plus, seeing a path away from my own mess seemed impossible because I was always on edge, putting out fires on the home front daily. My reality was that I was repeating what I had learned in my own family of origin (FOO). Having grown up in a different type of dysfunction, I learned to survive in chaos early in life and just kept going. I even believed that I was a super badass because of it. Little did I know I was just good at dealing with turmoil. Even though I realized I was repeating the pattern, I was never taught how to escape it. Therefore I had to learn that one all on my own. Sadly, this type of repetitive cycle must stop, or it continues generationally and negatively affects brain development. Childhood adversity accounts for over 30% of anxiety disorders and is strongly associated with emotional and behavioral dysregulation later in life (Bremner, 2008). I knew better, and in the end, I just couldn't knowingly do that to my children.

Are you curious about the turning point? Like many people, I wish I had done things more quickly, but that isn't who I am. I am slow and methodical, but I get the job done, eventually. Gradually I was able to put it all together for myself. Maybe I needed to continue learning lessons, or perhaps I wasn't in a position to understand how bad the chaos around me was. No one can while living in constant turmoil, we become too acclimated, it's our normal. Much like the frog sitting in a pot of water, I never noticed I was slowly beginning to boil. As awful a fate as that sounds, it's true, and most people don't realize when life is bad, so they just keep going until they no longer can. Something needs to hit them hard to wake them from their malaise, to force change and do something different. You have to jump!

Fortunately for me, I had learned all of the different theories and methods while I was in graduate school to help people therapeutically. Even though I knew being a therapist was my true calling, I also knew that I was searching for answers when I decided to become a therapist. I thought I would be able to heal myself, my family, and maybe even be able to fix my marriage. I could be a slow learner, or perhaps the crap I've lived through is so ingrained in me that I had to work extra hard to figure out a way to help myself navigate my emotions and trauma. Was I just completely broken as a person? I mean, I had gone to school and learned the techniques, but I still couldn't manage to find happiness and peace. Would I ever find the answers?

I tried using what I learned. I even read plenty of self-help books but couldn't seem to figure it out. I had to go much deeper than "let it go!" Have you ever read the books that suggest this ludicrous idea? I mean, holy shit, why wasn't this working? I had written down what I wanted to let go of and burned it in a commonly suggested ritual. I even wrote it all out and put it in balloons, releasing them to the universe. Letting it go wasn't working for my patients or myself; I was getting flustered by it all. I felt like a fraud. Not only was I not walking the walk, I now didn't believe the talk I was talking. I was upset and thought that those damn self-help books, and I, needed a rewrite. Let it go! I can't help but laugh at this idea, I mean, seriously? Are we just going to decide these things will no longer pop up and cause issues in our lives? The answer is NO, not possible. First of all, our brains are not like computers, where content can simply be erased. We have triggers and ghosts that continually bring us back. When we least expect it, a smell, look, memory, or afternoon breeze brings us right back to a moment (we will explore the science behind this in Chapter 4 on mindfulness.) Did I mention social media? Ugh, that damn time hop on Facebook has almost sent folks over the edge. Letting things go just doesn't work. So, what does?

This is where self-care and mindfulness come in. Although the concept took me a minute to fully piece together, I can honestly say that it is effective. Using self-care, mindfulness techniques, and self-awareness, allows you to manage those ghosts and triggers in a way that helps you not to get caught off guard or thrown off your game. It's a practice that you have to work hard at, but once you find your way, you'll do it intuitively. That's why I call it, Intuitive Self Care, or (ISC).

We have all done things on an intuitive level to soothe ourselves, but you probably weren't aware that you were actually doing self-care. One of my peeps told me a story about how in the thick of her unhappy marriage, she would go home every night and get lost in YouTube beauty videos. It was a way for her to make herself feel better and relax. Without being conscious of its impact, she was coping as best she could. Similarly, I stumbled upon pressure washing and discovered it brought great relief. I knew it was fulfilling, and I wanted to do it again, but I didn't realize it was me finding a way to soothe myself. Looking at the things that have helped you in the past before you became mindful about it, shows us that self-care really is an intuitive process.

When I mention self-care, most people assume I'm talking about doing something for yourself that you may not do on a regular basis. Things like getting a massage, maybe a pedicure, perhaps even going on vacation or a night out with your partner or friends. Of course, I am a big fan of all self-care, but ISC is a tad different. It requires more effort in terms of being aware of self even when you aren't actively trying to relax or re-energize. ISC requires a more mindful way of living. You see, humans are social animals born with a clean slate, but over the course of our lives, we expand and grow as a result of external stimuli. We then become a totality of the relationships and experiences that make up our lives. The good, the bad, even the horrific, make up our reality. How we live, the stressors we experience, the relationships we have, absolutely everything impacts us. Some of these moments influence us more than others, but they make up the sum of who we are. Being aware of all these threads that make us who we are and being able to navigate our way using various acts of self-care is what ISC is all about.

If we are more aware of who we are and how we created some of our ideas, feelings, quirks, fears, and beliefs, we are then more capable of identifying what the best path for ourselves might be. The trick is being able to dig in and ask ourselves what our Knowns are. I call the accumulated crap that makes us who we are Knowns. However, you have to be able to establish what those Knowns are, which is where most of my people struggle. We are not always aware of them on a conscious level, which is why we have to assess and work toward change. It requires us to be able to fully engage in the analysis of self, which scares the hell out of most people. However, once you do it, you begin operating from a completely different level of consciousness.

Allow me to give a simple example of what a Known might be. Let's say that when you were five years old, you went to a family barbeque. You remember playing with your cousins, laughing and having a wonderful time. You saw your parents dancing and enjoying themselves as well, and it was a glorious day for everyone. All of the memories you take away from that barbeque will be positive. Let's say it happens to be the very reason you LOVE going to cookouts. You associate grilling steaks, music playing, and warm sunny days with pure happiness. This is a memory that you cherish and ultimately impacts how you live your life. It shapes you into being a barbeque LOVER! Chances are, you will be at summer parties, grilling and chilling your entire life.

Now let's think about the same situation but this time let's throw in a tiny wrench. In this scenario, you were bitten by the neighbor's dog just before leaving to go home. There is blood everywhere, and you are whisked away to the hospital because it looks as if your finger might not be completely attached. You're screaming, your parents are freaking out, and it completely changes the good vibes of the day.

As you grow up, the narrative is no longer about what a beautiful day you had but is now focused on your finger that still looks weird, and that ferocious dog that attacked you and almost tore off your entire hand. As an adult, you have a fear of dogs, and the smell of anything being grilled makes you nauseous. You also avoid family gatherings and can't stand to hear any music from the '80s because it triggers you, and you get highly anxious. Notice the amplification of the memory?

This is the perfect example of a Known but also an excellent snapshot of memory storage. Both scenarios enlist our brains to encode and process our memories. One has positive emotions, and the other has negative emotions attached. If they were neutral, they would quickly be forgotten. While they are both considered salient or emotionally charged, stressful, or arousing experiences activate pathways that form long term memories (Reto Bisaz, 2014). This is important because even though the first scenario could be stored in long term memory, it might need to happen a few more times to create a neuro pathway. Still, the second scenario is most likely going to get stored immediately.

The first scenario is pleasant and creates positive imagery. The second scenario encapsulates the role of our brains and how the fight or flight mechanism works. It affects our sense of self and even how our brains react, moving forward. We know that because of specific experiences, you react a certain way to various stimuli. In this case, it was a dog bite when you were five years old. The triggers that bring you back to something that started off being so much fun is now a horrifying incident that changed your life forever. As with scenario one, knowns can be positive, but the ones that are most likely to keep us stuck are the negative ones. By understanding your

Knowns, you can begin to understand self while also allowing you to navigate life in a much different way.

Let's break it down a bit further. If you understand why you fear dogs, you get the option of changing that perception of "I've always been afraid of dogs" to "I was bitten as a child and am scared of dogs because of an incident." This also allows you to connect triggers that were related to the incident. If you get uneasy or avoid going to family gatherings, you now understand why. You don't really dislike family gatherings; you had a bit of trauma during one and now associate the two.

Utilizing ISC, you get to change the narrative, or at least understand where these fears came from and decide if they are relevant for you at this time in your life. Many of us have belief systems stemming from information processed at early ages or during times of extreme stress. Both situations cause us to remember or perceive situations differently than we do as adults or when stressed.

In the next chapters, we will begin looking at the science behind some of the concepts I've mentioned. Yes, there is science behind it. We will start by discussing Knowns a bit further because they are not merely experiences. They are compiled from various areas in your life. You must be willing and able to identify them and examine them in a way that allows you to be completely self-aware. Once you have identified your Knowns, I encourage you to write them down so that you can go even further in the assessment process. This information will become an essential part of your owner's manual. Understanding where these Knowns come from will make the next steps even easier.

After Knowns, we begin looking at the root or origin. The root allows us to reflect on the Known differently than we had previously. We see with clarity, introspection, compassion, and empathy for self and others. Allowing us to change perspective and, ultimately, how we think, feel, believe, and live our lives. After we get you equipped with this info, we can then start to look at mapping or connecting the threads in everyday life. This portion is a bit easier to accomplish because you will start noticing how it all intertwines, especially when we throw in mindfulness. Mindfulness is going to play a massive part in developing the skills necessary to live in an intuitive state of mind. All of the dynamics are going to work together with being mindful of self.

The final portions of ISC are going to require us to examine what being vulnerable means. Vulnerability is essential to being mindful. It will truly allow you to determine what you need to do to take care of yourself. At this point, we will create a list of self-care items to help us navigate our way. Without having developed the self-care items, you will continue to get stuck, so this piece is essential and is probably the most enjoyable.

Lastly, we will discuss energy and ask ourselves, who do we want to be? Are you aware of your energy? It turns out our outward energy is very much an aspect of how people respond to us. Remember how I mentioned Dr. Lentz's energy being so calm? Imagine if he had been frenzied that morning? I probably would have felt right at home because of my chaotic life at the time, but I also wouldn't have been curious or found value in what he was saying. He wouldn't have been walking the talk. This leads to the question about who we want to be. If we drop all of the negativity and release the crap, who are we? This can be a curious question for those of us who have identified as a survivor or victim. We create personas that follow the ideas and beliefs we have created throughout our lives based on our relationships and experiences. Once we are no longer defined by those things, who are we?

The benefit of doing all of this work is to be able to create an Owner's Manual. That's right; you will finally have instructions. Instead of just being told you should let go of the crap that is holding you back and just move on with life, I'm going to help you illuminate it in such a way that you begin to maneuver around it like an enlightened soul armed with knowledge and confidence. Without sounding too New Age-y, ISC will help you own your shit but not let it continue to interfere with life.

As for me, I couldn't continue not being authentic, so I put one foot in front of the other and figured out what to do. Ultimately, I gained momentum, putting the pieces together like a puzzle. I learned what would change my life forever. I'm happy to report that my mission now is teaching others to do the same. Luckily for me, I have a bit of a platform to teach and a mini-lab that allows me the opportunity to see others in their struggles as well as watch them make changes that profoundly turn things around for them. Talk about satisfying; there is nothing better than watching someone break free from what has kept them prisoner. It's like watching a beautiful butterfly discover their wings and take flight. It's magnificent to see the transformation. Not just because I know the path but because seeing a person happy, or content in life, and knowing they now have tools to navigate life more productively is deeply satisfying. I always tell my peeps that I am going to help them with their journey. Even if I haven't followed the exact course, I still know the escape route.

Are you ready to make changes that will profoundly impact your level of satisfaction with life?

Knowns & Beliefs

"We can never obtain peace in the outer world until we make peace with ourselves."

— Dalai Lama

I think of our Knowns as tethered balloons that follow us around. Sometimes they are on strings so long that they are challenging to see. Other times they are right near our heads, always there, no matter which way we turn. It's necessary to be accountable for all of them. Think of it as taking inventory of your crap. Figure out where it's flying so that you can readjust and get those Knowns in line and definitely out of sight. When I described this metaphor to one of my peeps, she joked with me that she felt like sometimes one of her balloons is always stuck to her head, causing her hair to stick straight up from the static electricity. She has since found relief from that pesky balloon, but she worked hard to move it further back and out of her hair. Without making changes, those balloons/Knowns don't ever go away, but we can keep them in check so that they no longer have power over us or our hair.

Before we go further, I want to look at the difference between a Known about self and a false or limiting belief. Often they intertwine and it becomes difficult to unravel them completely. Both can impact us profoundly, but it's essential to understand the difference. A Known is an experience that punctuates our life stories, perhaps becoming a part of who we are, marking turning points, closing options, and changing life directions (Cordon, 2004). Belief systems are built on our world views, many of which are passed on to us by our families, community, and culture. The beliefs that we learn usually do well for us until they become limiting or even cause damage (Sisgold, 2013). A false or limited belief is more along the lines of something you identify as or created for yourself but isn't true. I have heard people say that they aren't good at relationships and think it is a Known. Well, not exactly. Assuming you're not good at relationships, and will, therefore, never be in a good relationship, is a belief you have created. When we evaluate that statement, the belief has been created by a negative view or life experience. Unfortunately, if we believe it to be true, we tend to make it so. Ever hear of a self-fulfilling prophecy? When these beliefs go unchallenged, they can easily become our truth. Usually, these beliefs are based on a negative thought or emotion connected to distress, anxiety, fear, depression, or grief. The fact that you haven't had a successful relationship is the Known, and you should work hard at identifying the reason. It could be based on your family of origin never having modeled a good relationship for you, or perhaps you had an early experience with an abusive partner that made you

23

skittish about picking partners constructed on the fear of choosing a bad partner again. It is not, however, established on fact.

A false or limiting belief can come from anywhere but resonates with the idea that the negative thoughts that come into your mind are real. Can you imagine thinking every thought you have is true? It sounds absurd, but the reality is that without the ability to distinguish between false/limiting beliefs and reality, we create a destructive mind state. I see this all the time with super negative people. Nothing, and I mean nothing, changes their stance on certain things because their worldviews are so incredibly limited. When this happens, it makes life quite difficult for their pessimistic minds, and they struggle to think rationally. They experience anger, disconnection from others, and insecurities, which can ultimately contribute to depression and anxiety. We all have to remember that negative feelings and emotions are a necessary part of life, but we must identify and sift through them, so they don't take over. According to Steve Sisgold, "false and limiting beliefs are like parasites: they stay inactive in the mind until some thought or event triggers their response. Then they impede people's ability to think sensibly and rationally, and they affect perceptions and perspectives in a pernicious manner" (Sisgold, 2013).

Understanding that a false belief is not the same as a Known boils down to whether or not you only believe it to be true. Ask yourself, where did this belief come from? Is the belief helping you in any way, or is it fear-based? Is it supported by real-world experience, or is it just a random emotion or feeling? Another way to determine if it's real is to look for a root cause. Did the dog bite you, or did it just bark at you, therefore, leading you to believe it would bite you? Just thinking something can be dangerous because you are usually not open to the possibility that it isn't true: all dogs bark, but not all dogs bite. Opening up to new possibilities allows us to have new experiences that can help us redefine those negative beliefs.

Since many of our false beliefs are handed down to us by family, they could be just about anything in terms of family beliefs or even superstitions. One I remember vividly is something my mother told me when I was young and carried with me for years, was that I didn't like cheese. Seriously, for the longest time, I thought I didn't like cheese and was afraid it might make me sick. I assumed that because of the way my Mom would curl her nose in disgust when she talked about it, I mean, surely it had to be awful. It turns out, I do like cheese. In fact, I love cheese. It's my Mom who doesn't like cheese. This is a classic example of a belief that was handed to me. Every time I fix something with cheese in it, especially if my Mom is around, I remind her and retell the story to anyone in the room. I may still be a little mad about it too. Although, this one may be a bit more about having a funny story and teasing my Mom than anything else. It still fits the criteria of a false belief.

What are some false or limiting beliefs you grew up with?
How have they affected you?
Do you recognize any false or limiting beliefs that you may have
created for yourself?

Now that we have differentiated between beliefs and Knowns let's turn our attention to trauma. Trauma is going to be a major contributor to your Knowns. No one likes to discuss it, but it has to be addressed, given the amount of trauma people have experienced. Not long after I began working with people who have experienced trauma, I realized how much their brains are conditioned to respond to certain stimuli (Bremner, 2008). Of course, I had read about it and even researched it for over a year for my graduate research project. However, nothing prepares you for seeing it first-hand. Since so many of my people have experienced varying forms of trauma, I get to see its effects all the time. In spite of this, when I realized I was doing the same thing, I was somewhat taken back. Regrettably, I responded to my husband the way I would have responded to my abusive ex-husband. I caught myself and thought, "wow, that's some serious conditioning." First off, I felt terrible that it had happened and apologized profusely to him. Then I started to get a bit excited because I knew I was mindful enough to catch it. Even still, it had happened, and I needed to put in more effort to change myself and ultimately recondition my responses. I had to learn how to identify my old wounds to start fresh. I needed to make it my new response, and it had to become intuitive.

Uncovering and coming to grips with your Knowns/beliefs takes time and effort. We have to be honest with ourselves and allow those realities to be brought to the surface. We have to enable realizations that are sometimes hard to live with, but they identify who we are as people. They also allow us to create a path away from the Knowns/beliefs that wreak havoc or torture us throughout our lives.

Renee

Discovering your Knowns/beliefs is not an easy task, especially when you're determined to keep them hidden away. I experienced this with Renee, a woman who came in at the urging of her family. When Renee showed up, she wanted me to believe she was fine and was coping perfectly. She wasn't even sure why her husband and family insisted she see a therapist. It turns out, Renee had been suffering from bipolar disorder, among other things. She was medicated, although her mania was not in check, which made therapy difficult. Being bipolar itself is not problematic, especially when a person has found a way to maneuver through and take responsibility for their disorder, whether it be with medication or other options. Mania makes things much more difficult if it is not being treated appropriately. Renee's mania consisted of sleeplessness, grandiose thoughts, an altered sense of self and reality, overspending, acting out inappropriately in multiple areas of life, and racing/obsessive thoughts. She was all over the place.

Once we were able to get Renee properly diagnosed and medicated, she began to trust me, and we started to make progress unpacking those Knowns. Renee had an interesting life; her parents split early, and her father remarried soon after. They had the usual split household arrangement. He offered a stable home environment for Renee. In contrast, the home she shared with her mother was quite the opposite. Renee's mom had severe mental illness and continuously created chaos for Renee and her dad's family. Regrettably, she says she had to raise her mother and wasn't given a real childhood. Renee tried her best to escape the drama-filled landscape at her Mom's house. Needless to say, the standards at Mom's house were very different from those at Dad's.

As a child, Renee experienced lots of trauma but kept most of it secret. She was sexually molested by a family member and dealt with that trauma by doing what many survivors do; she ate to insulate and protect herself. Her thought process was that if she weren't physically appealing, no one would hurt her. As the years passed, Renee began to distance herself from her family because she felt different. Her weight had increased significantly, and she withdrew further from life. She created a false belief that she wasn't loveable or wanted. A message fostered along by her mother's many partners and husbands who never stuck around.

In an attempt to create normalcy, she married her high school sweetheart. They made a life for themselves and seemed happy for several years. Unfortunately, one stormy day changed all that Renee had worked so hard to achieve. She was raped at gunpoint in her own home. The details are horrendous, and she actually kept it a secret from everyone, even her husband, for several months. Even after beginning therapy, it took a couple of years for her to divulge the full details. Given Renee's past, she chose to keep it a secret, much like many of the other events in her life. Unfortunately, when she finally told her story, she was questioned by her husband and even her doctor. Her acting out after the rape was so unlike her, that no one understood what was going on. This major life event was so traumatic that it triggered her bipolar disorder. Her marriage ultimately ended, and she became estranged from her father and the family she cherished so much. Life was turned upside down. The aftermath of that event began her spiral into chaos, but also launched her journey into what she considers to be a true awakening.

For someone who has experienced as much trauma as Renee, it seems that identifying a list of Knowns/beliefs is a bit of a task. There are several, many are connected. However, she has done it masterfully. I couldn't be more proud of her and all that she has accomplished. She began by figuring out how her early years affected her. She then went on to traumas as a young person, and finally, she was able to tackle the rape. We were able to see how so much of her life wove in and out of the events she experienced, shaping her beliefs that ultimately created a person even Renee didn't recognize. From her relationships to her self-worth, body image, and more, Renee was able to find peace with who she was and heal from the trauma using self-care and mindfulness.

Having traumatic events such as Renee's is only one type of Known. Other Knowns can be experiences that shape you as a person, alter life's course, eliminate choices, denote turning points, or prolonged periods of extreme distress. Examples of these things include being in a bad car accident, breakups with friends or partners, a loved one dying, losing your home to a fire or natural disaster, being displaced or homeless, alcoholic parents, sick or ailing family members. The list could go on exhaustively. Depending on several factors like your age, emotional development, the influence of others around you during the event, resiliency, and even belief systems, you may or may not have residual effects. No experience is too small to have left a mark, and only you know what is causing problems for you.

Once you're able to understand what your Knowns are, you can then begin the process of healing. The way we heal is by seeing the Known in real-time and recognizing how it affects us. This requires us to become mindful of the triggers associated with the Known. Our brains are great at maintaining memories. If they weren't, this would not be necessary. Since they are, we need to know what our crap is. We need to understand its origin so that we can see how it affects us today. You might not have been as affected by a breakup when you were 14 unless it validated feelings about your parent's divorce and resulted in you believing that all men are terrible and can't be trusted. This is life-changing for some people. You might believe that men are the enemy and decide you'll never date, you should be alone forever, or you need to punish all the men you date. Whatever the process or belief you create, you need to understand where the idea came from so you can look at it through a different lens.

At 14, you had no real-world experience, only the pain of watching your parents go through a nasty divorce. You may not even know the entire story, but you think you have it all figured out. The hurt, anger, and confusion may have completely led you to a conviction that now shapes your world. Fast forward 20 years, if you revisit the situation with facts, a new understanding of how the world works, and a realization that 14 year olds have a limited perspective, you might see things a tad differently.

Similarly, small events can cause problems too. Let's say you were in a fender bender at the age of 40. Afterwards, you notice when you're driving, and get close to other vehicles, you hear the sound of metal crashing. It doesn't register at first, but gradually you notice that you're driving less often. You see a news report about safety concerns for a specific model of car, and even though you don't drive that car, you begin worrying. You take the story as absolute truth and decide that driving is too dangerous. Now you only walk or take a bus if it's an absolute emergency.

This minor accident has now morphed into something else. If we unpack what else was going on during this time, we realize that you were under a considerable amount of stress at work. Your girlfriend broke up with you, and your dog is sick. Somehow you link all of these to the accident because they all happened within a month of the accident. If we look at this situation and understand the circumstances, we see how a belief has been formed. You ultimately decide that cars are dangerous based on things that happened together but have no connection other than timing. If we look more closely at the circumstances we see that you and your girlfriend had broken up four times already, your dog got sick because your baby niece fed it chocolate, and work stress is seasonal because you are an accountant.

You certainly may have been nervous when driving after an accident because that is a normal response. If you experience many stressors in a short period, you might create a false belief around which you shape your life. By retracing the events and identifying the cognitive distortions, you can understand that you need to do a better job of stress management and keeping your perception in check. You need to be mindful that when overwhelmed, you create detrimental beliefs.

This is what I mean by creating your list of Knowns/beliefs. Your known crap, the stuff that created you, the things that helped you navigate your way through life, some can be wonderful, and some can be horrifying. Either way, they are what makes you, you.

After you do the work of determining your Knowns/beliefs, you can decide if the memories are accurate and help you make your way through life or, if the memories and ideas created about the event are skewed and have misdirected you. It's ok to know this as a problem area for you, and it may always be an uncomfortable situation with triggers. However, it is what you decide to do about those memories or triggers that will help you heal.

Looking back at Renee, howling wind was a big trigger. As on the day of her assault, her body responds with fear when she hears wind blowing. This is a normal response and one we expect from trauma victims. What Renee has learned to do is acknowledge her fear. When she hears the wind, she reminds herself that it can be a trigger, so she does extra self-care. She grounds herself by being aware of her surroundings and staying present. Sometimes this involves talking to someone about it or being at home in what she calls her blanket burrito to feel cozy and safe. She'll watch Disney movies, and sometimes she'll color or paint. Whatever she decides to do, she breaks out her list of self-care items and gets busy because she knows that otherwise, she might spiral into an episode of depression or mania. Renee has become a self-care/mindful ninja.

What are some of your Knowns?

How have they impacted you?

Root Causes

"We cannot solve our problems with the same thinking that created them."

— Albert Einstein

Now that we have described Knowns and false or limiting beliefs, we can begin work on the root causes. I like to focus on the root causes because people are more able to reflect on their Knowns or beliefs and begin redirecting when they understand where it comes from. This step is important because often you'll notice a repeat, or recycling, of your Knowns/beliefs. Meaning, you will see them come up over and over throughout the years. Often, the root cause of several issues is ultimately the same. Once you achieve this new perspective, you will more deeply understand why and how you created these ideas for self.

Once we identify the root cause, we then ease our minds by grounding ourselves into our current situation. By reminding yourself that you react to X because of something that happened when you were 12, you can decide if you want to respond from the stand-point of the 12-year-old who was unable to handle the situation. You can further explore this by soothing yourself and deciding to respond differently.

Does this sound easy? Well, don't get flustered just yet. Allow me to give an example of how these root causes work. Let's say you witnessed your parents fighting all the time as a child. You vividly remember waking up in the middle of the night on several occasions and listening from your bed to your parents fighting mercilessly. You probably didn't do, or say, anything because you were too scared. Except on one particular night, you heard your father scream that he was leaving, so you jumped out of bed and ran to find out what was happening. You found your dad, sitting on the porch with a suitcase. Cautiously you asked where he was going, but he said not to worry. He sent you back to bed, saying everything would be fine. At five years old, you followed directions because, really, what else could you do but cry?

So, you went back to bed but couldn't sleep for trying desperately to hear what else was happening, as if you could possibly control the situation. Finally, exhausted, you fell asleep when the screaming subsided. Then you woke up terrified about what happened while you slept. You ran out of your room and found everyone sleeping soundly. Dad was in bed too. Everything seemed to be okay, catastrophe was avoided, for now.

Seeing these things happen regularly as a child sets up a cycle of panic and relief. Panic because your foundation is never completely solid. Everything could blow up at any minute, and you don't know what changes that would bring. You have a false sense of relief because, while there is palpable trouble in your family, you think it will be okay, especially if you are paying close attention at all times. You develop a false sense of control by becoming hyper-vigilant.

Let's look at how this may become problematic as you get older. As you age, you have trouble in relationships. You're always worried about your partner cheating because it turns out, that's what the majority of those fights were about between your parents. Therefore, you got the message as a child that people cheat even if they love you. This message is obviously flawed, but it is what you learned from experience. We call this "modeled behavior." We learn how to be in relationships from our parents and we often, but not always, repeat things we saw in our FOO.

It's a false belief that you can control things if you are hyper-vigilant, paying close attention to details. I often see people do this after experiencing infidelity. They strongly believe they can keep their partners from straying if they become detectives. This misplaced attempt at controlling a partner is utterly exhausting. Besides, do you really want to keep this behavior up forever? Good relationships are based on trust; living through the rollercoaster of a faithless partner, let alone watching a parent cheat, is traumatizing. To think you must constantly be hypervigilant, control your surroundings, is no way to live. Beyond exhaustion, it causes stress, anxiety, depression, and yes, PTSD.

Still, another issue can be the feeling that the other shoe is about to drop. This leads to worry and concern. I've seen people begin isolating and detach from those they love because they are so concerned about what could happen. They may not sleep or sleep well because they worry all the time.

All of these issues, and a plethora of others, have a single root cause. They are all related to those experiences as a child when you were learning how to live in your environment. Your chaotic environment shaped you, and now you struggle to trust your partner, can't sleep soundly, constantly worry about things beyond your control, try to control all aspects of your life, or simply give up controlling anything because you are frozen with fear. You had bad modeling, and now these issues are wreaking havoc on your life.

Once you work backward and figure out the root of these issues, you can begin healing. Have you ever had a bad dream where you woke up totally freaked out? When you start to process the dream you realize you watched a scary movie about Zombies, then had a discussion with a friend about some weird ghost story they heard as a child, you also saw some strange artwork that reminded you of an aunt whose house smelled like cotton candy and cat pee, then finally you realize that you ate mushrooms for dinner and that always makes you have odd dreams.. You analyze that scary dream until you understand where all the pieces originated from and laugh at yourself, marveling at your brain's awesome ability to put together various parts of your day and, even though scrambled up, it was kind of cool. Ultimately you feel relieved because you understand where it all came from — even the cat pee!

Understanding the root cause of your issues is similar to figuring out those weird dreams. You can think back to the root of those issues and ask yourself if it's happening now. What would you do differently as an adult? You can also take care of your inner child who suffered some deep shit, reminding yourself that you are ok, and no longer have to be scared. You also get the opportunity to forgive and decide not to allow those old experiences to be the story you keep living. You get to decide to stop operating from those wounds and find the strength to create new truths for yourself. Those old experiences do not have to control us or dictate who we are, even if we carry them with us.

Find the relief in understanding where some of your beliefs, tendencies, and pain come from and then challenge yourself to do something different. This isn't easy, but it is so worth it as you become more and more aware of self. You can then intuitively begin deciding who you want to be and not a slave to your past. Just like that nightmare, you sigh with relief when you understand why you're getting upset.

Ellie

One of my peeps, named Ellie, is a great example. Ellie was severely abused as a child. Her mother let her know from the start she wasn't wanted. Ellie's mom told her she was just another mouth to feed, but it was good that she had her so she could help with her siblings. Ellie reports that she was never shown love or affection. Sadly, the only time she can remember getting attention was when she was being beaten. Her mother always told her she would never amount to anything and expected her to "get knocked up" and bring shame to her family. As soon as she was able to get out of her house, she ran. She met a boy and, of course, soon found herself pregnant. She married the boy because she couldn't let her mother be right.

Ellie didn't engage with her mother for many years because she was ashamed of getting pregnant. She always thought if she could be happy in her marriage, and raise a happy child, she would prove her mother wrong. This was a major goal for Ellie, although she struggled with finding happiness within herself. She always felt less than because she had come from a poor family, and her husband was from a wealthy family that seemed to be perfect. She soon found out things aren't always as they appear. Her husband had a problem with alcohol that worsened over the years. Ellie struggled to keep things together, but she did. When her child was diagnosed with Leukemia, she was devastated. Her husband told her in a drunken rage that they shouldn't ever have had their daughter, she was a mistake that God was trying to fix. Ellie heard those words and left him.

I am pleased to report that her daughter's cancer was treated, and she has been cancer-free for 15 years. However, Ellie still struggles with her past. She came to me because she remarried, but her new husband recently told her she wasn't cutting it, and he wished she was more like his deceased wife. She fell apart because she felt less than again. Her doctor diagnosed her with depression and sent her to me after months of being on meds that didn't help.

We started by unpacking all of her crap and, I must admit, it was a lot. However, once we understood the root cause of her feelings, she began to feel better. She had to understand that her mother set this in motion by not only mistreating her, but also making her feel less than, or unwanted. We discussed how that impacted her as a mother, and she realized she did better by showing her child unconditional love and constant care. We also helped her wrap her head around her ex-husband and see him in a new light. You see, he never learned coping skills from his FOO and felt great pressure from an overbearing father. He drank to numb the pain and, unfortunately, for Ellie, that pain was fused with the illness of their child. Neither of them had the tools, or support system, to handle what was happening to their family, especially at the tender age of 23.

When Ellie began to put the pieces together and see things differently, she realized she was terrified to love because she felt unlovable. When her new husband mentioned that he loved how his deceased wife made fried chicken, Ellie lost it. He hadn't actually told her she wasn't cutting it; he just mentioned to his kids that he missed those Sunday dinners and that awesome fried chicken that no one else knew how to cook. Ellie took it as a slap in the face, because she heard her mother saying she was useless, and no one would ever love her.

What a journey. This woman was carrying her pain around like it happened yesterday. When she finally put it all together, it was a true light bulb moment. She sobbed while her husband comforted her. They saw each other differently that day. It was amazing to be a part of the process but, even more, that Ellie was able to understand where those ideas came from and how she was susceptible. She is still actively working on being mindful of her past and how it affects her. She comes in now and then and always tells me how long a tether her "Known" balloons are on. She works to keep the Knowns as far away as possible, but every now, and then they get a little too close, and she says she feels them, but she knows what to do. Ellie has nearly mastered mindfulness and self-care. She is successfully living what she considers to be the best version of self.

I try to help all my peeps untangle the roots that keep them bound. We all have them, but once we recognize them, we can diffuse their power. We get to change our response; we understand it's a sore spot, but it doesn't define us. We get to shed some of the control these experiences have on us and move forward with our lives. We become mindful and less likely to fall back into the old belief patterns we created. Just like the nightmares that we break down and understand, then peacefully go back to sleep. We can continue living the lives we want to live when we untangle our Knowns.

Mindfulness

"Between stimulus and response, there's a space, in that space lies our power to choose our response, in our response lies our growth and our freedom."

— Viktor Frankl

Holocaust Survivor

A s a therapist, I like to consider myself to be eclectic in my use of therapies. It is common practice to utilize various theories to help a person based on who they are and what they need. However, I would have to say that Mindfulness Based Therapy (MBT) is my absolute go-to. I have yet to meet a person that can't benefit from the use of MBT. It's used in schools, hospitals, and the military to promote good mental and physical health. Beyond helping us live better, more satisfying, happier lives, research on mindfulness has shown that it helps with stress and anxiety reduction, emotional regulation, decrease in depression relapses, increased flexibility in responses, increased awareness, increased clarity, increased concentration, and improved relationships (Davis, 2011). There is plenty of empirical evidence to support the use of mindfulness, but I've seen it work first hand for my peeps and myself, which is why I am such an advocate.

In addition to improving our quality of life and overall wellbeing, mindfulness has been found to reduce symptoms of many disorders, including anxiety, depression, substance abuse, eating disorders, and chronic pain (Holzel, 2011). Mindfulness is also incredibly effective in helping with stress, worry, and rumination, which can ultimately lead to the development of mental illness (NIMH, n.d.). Given the abundant research that has been established, it is safe to say that mindfulness is a useful tool in helping us gain self-control, which is what most, if not all, of my patients are looking for. So how did mindfulness become so valuable? Actually, it's been around for thousands of years with people practicing it on its own or as part of a larger tradition. Mindfulness is found in many religions but originates in Buddhism and Hinduism. The word mindfulness is said to be a simple translation for Sati, which is the Buddhist term for enlightenment. Therefore, it is not much of a stretch to get from today's terms of self-control and self-awareness to that of becoming enlightened. It's been a way to practice self-awareness throughout the ages and is seen by many as a way to develop self-knowledge and wisdom. Utilizing such power for oneself is exactly what ISC is about.

Now let's discuss the meaning of mindfulness. I often ask my people if they know what it is, and while they have heard the word, they don't quite understand the concept. Mindfulness is often referred to as self-regulation, the state of being aware, being in the present moment, and a way of processing information (Davis, 2011). All of these fit the collective ideology of mindfulness, but for the benefit of learning, I would like to narrow it down a bit to becoming aware of yourself and your environment. It is the practice of noticing your thoughts, feelings, and physical sensations, all without applying judgment. Non-judgment is key. Mindfulness requires us to consciously direct our awareness moment by moment because it is set in the present.

Throughout my years as a therapist, I kept noticing a common issue with many of my patients. The problems are different; however, the common factor in these problems always comes back to understanding, not only the cycles that help manifest and maintain these problem areas, but also an ability to self-regulate, or do self-care, during times of crisis or when problems start to flare. When we self-regulate, we are simply readjusting to a stimulus that throws us off. Think in terms of an HVAC system that corrects the temperature setting when it heats up outside. To achieve homeostasis, the HVAC system kicks on the air conditioning, thus returning the environment to the desired temperature. We do this as human beings when we are hungry, we eat. If we are tired, we sleep. We self-regulate to achieve an optimal setting.

Are you aware of your environment?
How do you feel?
What do you need to reach homeostasis?

Many of my peeps have learned to self-regulate using self-care whenever they feel anxiety, depression, or any other state of unease. In doing so, they demonstrate their understanding of how to take care of themselves. We all have problems, and we always will, but understanding what to do and how best to take care of ourselves when these problems arise, helps keep them from escalating. This is where mindfulness comes into play. If we are aware of ourselves, we can make different choices, so we don't get sucked into the vacuum associated with our Knowns/beliefs. If I know that watching scary movies freaks me out and I can't sleep for days after seeing one, I'm not going to watch one the night before a big test, or for that matter, ever. Being mindful, you would consider the consequences of watching the scary movie. It's as simple as planning ahead, but it goes much further.

When I begin working with someone, I slowly start to pull back the curtain to the magical land of mindfulness. It's not difficult to learn, and once you begin practicing, you will get better and better. I think of mindfulness as a way of seeing the world. Through a mindful lens, you see your environment, but you become aware of yourself at the same time. We all see things differently and have different perceptions of what is going on around us. When you are mindful, you consider how things are going to affect you as a person. For instance, if I walk into a room and there is stressful energy or tension, I know that my body is going to respond in a stressful manner due to having been in an abusive relationship. It could be anything that signals my brain to bring those memories flooding back, that's what our brains do. It's like a warning system, but it's a protective system too. Either way, my body will respond, my blood pressure may elevate slightly, my shoulders tense, or my face will flush. At this point, I need to be mindful of these reactions and self-regulate. After years of practicing mindfulness, self-regulation, and self-care, I know exactly what to do to take care of myself.

There are steps to learning to be mindful. When learning how to be mindful, self-regulate, and do self-care, start by simply paying attention to your surroundings. What gets you stressed out? Who gets you going and why? Are there places that cause you to feel tension? I want my people to begin slowly so that they understand what is affecting them. Look at simple things that you know cause you stress. Write them down because they will be important elements of your owner's manual. They can be small things like figuring out what to have for dinner and gradually move up to things like meeting work deadlines or seeing a person that you have conflict with. Write them all down. Even the littlest of things may be causing you problems.

What are we looking for? Look for normal signs of stress like sweaty palms, knots or butterflies in your tummy, tensed shoulders, the urgent need to urinate, or even heart palpitations. Everyone has different ways of feeling stress or tension. Knowing what symptoms you are susceptible to will be an important way to navigate this first step, so give it some thought. I've had people describe interesting symptoms that aren't common, like odd smells or fingertips getting cold. So, pay close attention. Again, write these down so that you can utilize them in your owner's manual. You may notice it changes over time, but that's ok because if we are aware of our body signals, we can be more active in self-regulating. We will learn more about identifying your stress cycle in chapter 6.

After writing down the stressors and figuring out what your signals are, we are ready to connect the stressors to some of our Knowns. I do not suggest trying to figure this out overnight. It takes time and you will get overwhelmed by the process if you try to do it all at once. This gradual process is also a way for you to feel in control. It takes time to truly be mindful. I've been at it for years and I still find new stressors or triggers. It makes me happy when it happens because I know I am growing as a person and I get to add to my owner's manual.

Connecting your Knowns and beliefs to stressors is important. Many times, I see people telling me stories about how mindful they are, but this situation happened, and they aren't sure what to do. Inevitably, we can connect it all back to a major Known. Once they take the time to do it, they get the "oh yeah" look on their faces; they commonly look relieved. What they thought was a major setback was really just a blip, usually related to their slacking on self-care.

Many stressors can come hurling at you in various situations, including old trauma, self-esteem issues, or just being tired. Combinations of these experiences can make you respond in either an appropriate or inappropriate way. The question is, which way will you respond? Let's say that I know because of my FOO issues; my first response may not be a good one. If I understand this and self-regulate, instead of having a negative reaction, I will have several options. My first option is to remove myself from the situation if I am not in a good place. I can also choose not to allow the energy or negativity to affect me. Either way, I have more control when I am mindful.

There's no harm in someone who is learning how to do self-care to decide to walk away. That, in and of itself, is the definition of self-care. As you grow stronger in your ability to be mindful and do self-care, you can then decide how, or if, you want to respond.

What makes me sad is that we don't just stop for a moment and examine what we are feeling; we aren't aware of our thoughts, or the environment surrounding us, let alone how our bodies are reacting. Most people don't think they have time to do so. It's not as if we don't want to be happier or live our best lives; it's something society doesn't greatly support. Being mindful only takes time when you first begin the practice; after a while, it becomes intuitive.

This leads me to my final portion on becoming mindful. It's about being in the moment. One of my first experiences with being in the moment dates way back to high school. I was in my car sitting at a traffic light rocking out to Bon Jovi on the radio. John and I were giving a fabulous concert for one when I happened to notice a friend in my rear-view mirror, laughing her ass off at me. Surprisingly I wasn't embarrassed, but I did laugh at the situation. As I pulled away, singing with a smile, I laughed because I realized that I had gotten lost in the music and how powerful that was. Losing yourself in something or being completely present feels great. I noticed that I wore that smile for a long time. I also felt relaxed and at peace.

Fast forward many years, and I noticed other times when I felt completely lost in a moment. When I would play with my babies, garden, pull weeds, or cook. I wasn't really aware that I was using these moments to survive the stress I was living under. It was an intuitive process, and I honestly wish I had been aware because I would have done it much more often. Having those "in the moment" times greatly reduces stress and anxiety. They add up like a savings account if you are mindful enough to be truly cognizant of and seek them out. I am a sucker for getting lost in a moment, seriously, I search for things that bring me joy. I noticed when I focus on seeking joy and looking for the positives in life, I am one happy girl.

> What makes you happy?
> Have you ever caught yourself smiling when you were busy doing something or thinking of a memory?
> Do you take the time to let it register that you are grinning or feeling positive?

Asking yourself multiple times throughout the day to focus on positives is another great way to be mindful. Looking for such positivity will help you learn to see the good instead of focusing on the crap. In fact, as soon as I am aware that I may be feeling crabby, I return to a more mindful state and look for the good. I also evaluate what knocked me off my game. I might be running late, or possibly I am feeling the inflammation related to my autoimmune disorder, but I bring myself back to a place of neutral with self-care activities. We will discuss what real self-care is about in the next section. Once I readjust, I am able to focus on the good. I also happen to like how my body feels when I am calm and at peace. It turns out, people respond to me better. I don't get flustered and the normal stress and strains of the day seem to be easier.

Below is an example of a mindfulness cycle. What questions do you need to ask yourself?

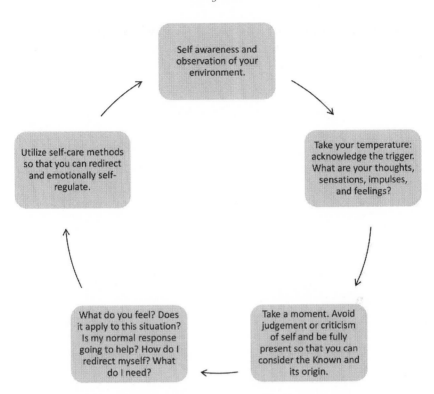

Self awareness and observation of your environment.

Take your temperature: acknowledge the trigger. What are your thoughts, sensations, impulses, and feelings?

Take a moment. Avoid judgement or criticism of self and be fully present so that you can consider the Known and its origin.

What do you feel? Does it apply to this situation? Is my normal response going to help? How do I redirect myself? What do I need?

Utilize self-care methods so that you can redirect and emotionally self-regulate.

Now that we have a working definition of mindfulness and an idea of how it works, we need to understand the science behind how our brains work. It's a bit technical, but I will break it down as simply as possible because I feel that if we understand how and why it's happening, we can be more aware and not get caught up in the process.

The Stress Response

When a stressor or threat comes at us, our brains respond by sending a signal to the amygdala. The amygdala is a limbic system structure that is involved with emotion, motivation, and is largely connected to survival. Emotions such as fear, anger, and pleasure are processed in this area in addition to memory storage, sorting, and consolidation. Memories that are particularly fear influenced are managed and formed in the amygdala. Consider the amygdala, the emotional processing center that helps encode and interpret memories (HHP, 2018). When the amygdala interprets a distress signal, it sends a message to the hypothalamus. The hypothalamus activates the pituitary gland, which then activates the adrenal glands. Hormones are secreted by the adrenal glands, which include adrenaline, noradrenaline, and cortisol. Together these hormones trigger the fight or flight response.

A number of physical changes are felt within the body as a result of the hormones triggering the fight or flight response. They include things like:

- Increased heart rate
- Increased breathing
- Increased blood pressure
- Increased blood glucose
- Feeling flushed
- Tunnel vision

All of these responses are normal and help us deal with real or perceived threats. However, when the fight or flight response is turned on repeatedly in the absence of danger, it becomes maladaptive and generates anxiety. When the amygdala is activated in the absence of an actual threat, the body has no outlet for the fight or flight response and is flooded with hormones that are not utilized. This can lead to an overload of cortisol, which can cause our amygdalae to become enlarged, which increases the panic, or fight or flight response. This increase is one of the reasons we feel anxiety all the time. We are essentially unable to turn it off because our amygdala is being hijacked (Moyer, 2019).

Unfortunately for us, our amygdalae are being hijacked on a regular basis. Past traumas are a contributing factor because they make us overly sensitive to triggers. It's a protective mechanism of the brain to process frightening memories and an attempt at preventing perceived danger. Consequently, when people are reminded of trauma, psychological cues cause us to re-experience the fear and cause the following symptoms:

- Intrusive thoughts
- Waking flashbacks
- Recurrent nightmares
- Intense emotional distress
- Rapid heartbeat
- Sweating
- Hyperventilation
- Muscle tension
- Dizziness
- Crying
- Shaking

Additionally, prolonged stress causes a similar response. Our brains get so overloaded with the busy lives that we live in a constant state of stress. How did we get to this place where we are all so stressed out we can't live our best lives? It's the fast-paced go, go, go world we live in today. In 2018 The American Psychiatric Association did an opinion poll about anxiety, the poll found that 39% of U.S. adults feel more anxious than they did a year ago even though we persistently glamorize being overworked, busy, and stressed (APA, 2018). It doesn't take a mental heavyweight to realize that stress and being busy is seriously affecting us.

I'm old enough to remember when we only had land lines. It's hard to believe, but it's true, we could actually leave the house without a tracking device on us. As weird and even scary, as that might seem, it was nice to be free to go about your day without being attached to a phone or computer. Can you imagine having time completely to yourself, where no one can reach you? In retrospect, it was glorious, but now we can scarcely imagine such a scenario.

Beyond our cellphones, we are doing more than ever before. We are all so busy that we don't have time to spare. We have 500 things to do today and a list a mile long for tomorrow. It's our new norm, and it's killing us.

Have you ever had sweaty palms, felt like your heart was going to pound right out of your chest, felt nauseated, or can't sleep at night? All of these symptoms, and many more, are influenced by cortisol, the stress hormone. These symptoms are so common anymore that many people assume it's normal. Luckily, practicing mindfulness helps decrease the size of our enlarged amygdala, it reduces our threshold for stress by reducing the production of cortisol and improves our reaction to stressful situations by creating new neuropathways (where and how memories are responded to) (Bergland, 2013). The restructured neuropathways allow the amygdala a chance to redirect the memories associated with fear, so those memories don't automatically hit the fight or flight button, causing panic. This is considered neuroplasticity, which is our brain's ability to change over our lifetime. Without changing those neuropathways by lowering our cortisol levels and eliminating chronic stress, we run the risk of increasing mental illness, decreasing our resilience, and life expectancy (Sapolsky, 2019).

Mindfulness is also incredibly effective in helping with stress, worry, and rumination, which can ultimately lead to the development of mental illness (NIMH, n.d.). Unless you are living off the grid, you know all about stress and how much it is affecting our lives these days. We aren't living the lives we want to live; we are simply getting through the day. It became clear to me from the sheer number of stress-related illnesses coming into my office that mindfulness needed to be taught to the masses. My approach thus far has been one person at a time, but my goal is to spread the word and teach as many people as I can.

Beyond our busy lifestyles, we also get stuck in our own ideas and beliefs that keep us unable to clearly see reality. This is influenced so heavily by our experiences and environment, that until we step outside ourselves and look at things through a different lens, we'll keep repeating the behavior and never truly learn the lesson at hand, or see things in a divergent manner. I'm happy to say that mindfulness is how we break past our experiences, environmental influences, beliefs, and ideas to carefully examine the contrasting perspectives. It's how we slow down and actually nurture ourselves.

Embracing Vulnerability

"Vulnerability is the birthplace of connection and the path to the feeling of worthiness. If it doesn't feel vulnerable, the sharing is probably not constructive."

— Brené Brown

I have a confession to make. Sometimes I get a kick out of watching people feel uncomfortable. I don't mean in a cruel way, but in that, "oh no, you are going to challenge me to do something that freaks me out" kind of way. I can always see it coming, and the facial expressions are priceless. A sure-fire way to get that uncomfortable response is for me to suggest they practice vulnerability. Lord have mercy, the faces I get with that request. The reason I get a kick out of it is that I know what they will gain, and it will be a glorious moment once they allow themselves to be vulnerable.

Why am I so excited about vulnerability? Mostly because of the impact it has on people's lives. Vulnerability is a crucial step to achieving self-actualization. Which is when an individual realizes their full potential and understands who they are as a person. In this section, you will notice that I use vulnerability interchangeably with susceptible. That's because they are similar, but I feel that in order for people to understand why vulnerability is good, they have to understand why it can be bad, so using an alternative word will help you digest the information and not get the two terms mixed up. The difference is about whether or not you are doing it mindfully. To fully achieve ISC, you must learn the difference and get comfortable identifying both forms.

Being vulnerable means open for potentially being physically or emotionally harmed. Being susceptible means you lack protection or power of resistance against something present or threatening. They may sound similar but are different. Think of it like this; our brains work in an amazing way to protect us at all costs. As we discussed in previous chapters, when we experience pain, trauma, or fear, our brains remember and create a path to avoid the pain. It's remarkable as a protective mechanism, but it also causes us to avoid anything resembling the original issue. That's why we avoid being vulnerable. Essentially, our brains create a new narrative that says hide and DO NOT let anyone in or know there is a chink in our armor. So, we do just that. Not showing vulnerability keeps us from getting hurt again, at least that's what our brains tell us. The problem is, it doesn't really work. It just keeps us from living a full life.

So, what does it mean to be vulnerable? It means showing emotions to others, opening up to things that might not go so well, trying something that scares the crap out of you, getting back on the horse after falling, or trusting people not to hurt you. Sound familiar? It should, if you haven't recognized this pattern for yourself, Brene Brown has been researching and writing about it for years. In her book, *Daring Greatly: How the Courage to Be Vulnerable Transforms the Way We Live, Love, Parent, and Lead* and in her very famous TED talk, *The Power of Vulnerability* she discusses all of the reasons why we are vulnerable, why it scares the crap out of us, and why its good for us. According to Brown, "vulnerability is basically uncertainty, risk and emotional exposure" (Brown, 2015). Trust me when I say, this statement couldn't be more accurate. Watching people sit in my office where they feel somewhat secure; they act like they are naked while exposing their true selves. It's amazing how many of my peeps can't even look at me while telling their truth. It's only when I don't respond like I am horrified, and then I normalize it do I get to see their shoulders lower, and the look on their faces moves from dread and fear to relief and appreciation. I think of this as my superpower. It's not really a power at all, but watching a person open up and feel the safety that vulnerability provides is absolute magic.

When are you vulnerable?
Have you ever allowed yourself to be emotionally exposed?
What happened?
Do you fear people knowing who you are? Why?

Since so many people are overly defensive about their flaws, hang-ups, quirks, and idiosyncrasies. They protect themselves so much that they are just going through life, closing themselves off to others, sucking up the pain, suffering in silence, and pushing down their feelings. It's often the only way they have been able to survive what they've been through. When I ask them to try something different, they freak out. However, I happen to know that healing comes with vulnerability. I also know joy is a result of vulnerability. You see, we need people, we need to be open to others, we need to have our moments when we are not 100%, we need to trust, and most of all we need to be authentic. Being real is an absolute must. Going out into the world and expressing ourselves authentically is difficult because we fear people will judge us, see our flaws, or simply not like, or approve of our authentic selves. Without being vulnerable, we carry a plethora of negative emotions, and there is absolutely no joy in negativity.

Now let's explore what being susceptible looks like. Consider this form of vulnerability in terms of being susceptible to an illness or contracting a disease. Many of my peeps have the tools they need to deal with their Knowns but often find themselves getting triggered and feeling they have slid back into whatever situation they first began working on. This is where being aware of self allows us to understand when we are susceptible, thus allowing us to determine what we need to do to help ourselves. Are you mindfully being vulnerable to open yourself up for growth, or are you unknowingly making yourself susceptible to old wounds or stressors? Think of it like this; I am reverting back to some old behavior. Why? What has me susceptible right now? What trigger is causing me to be scared?

Kara

One of my patients, Kara, worked for a couple of years battling debilitating depression, similar to what her father experienced. After digging in and creating the tools necessary to get relief, she felt great and was able to return to the life she had missed out on for years. About a year into her recovery, she took a new job that triggered her. She suddenly felt she'd fallen back into depression and would never outrun it again.

When she came in for her appointment, we discussed her feelings, and I reminded her that she had a tool belt full of useful tools for depression. When I asked her about being vulnerable, she was challenged because she had only considered depression as the culprit. She hadn't considered all of the things she was dealing with. As we began to unpack what she was feeling after her return to work, she realized that maybe her feelings were, in fact, frustrations, and a realization that she hadn't accepted her limitations. She was feeling overwhelmed, tired, and due to seasonal changes, she had less energy. She thought she should rev things up and become a busy bee, so she loaded her schedule with activities like she was unstoppable. She was going at full speed.

It wasn't until I asked about all the things she was doing that she realized she'd stacked the deck against herself. In reality, she was going back to using old habits without acknowledging she was vulnerable. Her susceptibility was that she had been oblivious to her needs. She didn't thrive on being busy all the time. Her job wasn't satisfying. The money she made was the only reason she was working, and there was no fulfillment. She tried to tell herself otherwise, but she wasn't being honest about what she needed to be her best self. She also forgot the self-care aspect of her treatment. She forgot to put the oxygen mask on herself first.

Once Kara recognized susceptibility as the real culprit, she was able to see how self-care fell to the wayside when she was triggered. The triggers are always going to be there in some capacity, but when she is susceptible or not doing self-care, her depressive symptoms are more likely to resurface. Therefore, Kara realized when she is susceptible, she needs to be vigilant about self-care. She also needs to understand what is really happening and not assume its always depression.

I see this with my patients frequently. When they feel distressed, they tend to assume it's depression or anxiety because that's been their experience, and they're afraid of going through it again. They are often unaware of other feelings or emotions that could be causing their discomfort. I call this the one-pot problem. Once a person has experienced depression or anxiety, that's the pot they put all their discomfort into, even though it's not always depression or anxiety. It's almost like after having strep throat, thinking that's what it is every time your throat hurts. The reality is that it could be many other things, but they convince themselves they have strep throat.

After helping Kara understand the rainbow of emotions it could be, she decided maybe she wasn't as depressed as she'd thought. She recognized she wasn't being aware of herself, and what she needed was self-care. She had simply forgotten her vulnerabilities. All of her emotions were signs that she had gone back to her old ways. Not only was depression a theme, but she also carried issues from her FOO. She had learned long ago that her mother, in particular, valued a certain lifestyle. The underlying message for Kara was that as long as things look pretty on the outside, and you surround yourself with perfection, all is right with the world. Kara had gone all-in when she was making changes to deal with her depression, including moving from an incredible house she had purchased many years prior. The pictures she shared with me were fantastic. Her house was decorated like it was about to be showcased in House Beautiful. Her home was gorgeous.

Everything was perfect, with nothing out of place. It was like a showroom or museum that is roped off.

As soon as I saw those photos, I remembered as a child how my mother always kept our house immaculate and perfectly decorated. Seriously, people would walk in our home and look a bit scared to touch anything. We had white carpet, and it looked like a Home-A-Rama staged home. We didn't live in that house. No one was allowed to be comfortable; it was a showpiece. Why? It was a way for my mother to make everything look perfect when it totally wasn't perfect…at all! Sound familiar? That's because it's precisely what Kara was doing with her home. She wanted everyone to focus on the beautiful surroundings, but DO NOT look behind the curtain. The façade needed to be maintained, and she did for as long as she could.

Unfortunately, I think this phenomenon is relatively common with many of us. We are taught not to air our dirty laundry or don't let people know too much of our business because they might use it against us. We don't want people to think badly of us, that would be heresy. I'm confident my mother learned this way of dealing with tough situations either from her FOO, or she figured it out and used it as a coping skill. Allowing yourself to be vulnerable is having the courage to be yourself, to experience risk and uncertainty. It also makes you human and will enable you to experience living in the moment and enables you to feel joy. It's like taking the mask off that most of us have always used to feel safe. I joke with my peeps that they often find ways to create facades to keep others from seeing the hot mess behind the curtain.

I say letting people see the mess makes more sense. Besides, it's too hard to keep the rouse going. These are things people do. We learn a way to deal with adversity, and we utilize the hell out of it. Often it's about survival. The thing is, we have to be able to look at this type of behavior and ask ourselves if it's helpful, or is it just continuing a bad habit? This is what self-actualization is all about. Do you truly know who you are and why you do things? Are you being protective, and what would it look like to instead be vulnerable?

As you can see with Kara, there are two sides to vulnerability. Kara was vulnerable by being susceptible because she wasn't doing self-care, and inevitably her symptoms of depression resurfaced. She also had to be vulnerable by letting her guard down and not using the façade she had created to protect herself. She needed to be okay, not making life look like everything was perfect. Her new house wasn't perfect, so she had to be comfortable being uncomfortable. She is still learning who she is, but she can proudly tell you she isn't PERFECT!

Both forms of vulnerability are essential for us as human beings, and we have to be sure to be aware of each meaning of this complex word. So, you might ask me why I want people to be vulnerable and still be mindful of their susceptibilities? The answer is that without vulnerability, we aren't able to experience the courage to be ourselves and therefore live in joy. We're overprotecting ourselves when we prevent ourselves from becoming vulnerable because we think we can't afford to let people in or let people know what's going on. Kara likes to remind me that I teased her a bit when she first started coming to see me because I told her she was ripe for the picking when she asked how I got her to let things out so easily. The truth is, she was in such a protective mode that she was ready to explode. She had been holding all of the pain and anxiety in for so long it had nowhere else to go. As a seasoned practitioner, I could feel her energy. It was palpable.

She needed to be vulnerable emotionally, to let her pain out, and stop trying to be perfect for everyone around her. Once she started being vulnerable, discussing it, and allowing herself to not be the ideal wife, mother, daughter, sister, and employee, she was able to begin healing. The fragmentation of self that happens when you are not vulnerable was halted. Kara began to feel whole and, most importantly, she felt joy. Even though she had good moments in life, joy had often escaped her. Through this process, Kara became her authentic self.

Being vulnerable is also about letting people in. This is quite difficult for those of us who have been hurt deeply by the hand of someone we loved or trusted. I don't know many people who have gone through life without heartbreak. At some point, we feel this pain, and for many of us, it becomes our calling card. The old "I'm not good at love, so I will just be alone forever" mentality is one that I hear often. This is yet another attempt at self-protection. It's usually more comfortable than going through the trouble of evaluating what's really happening with our lives. Either we need to look long and hard at ourselves, or we need to completely re-evaluate how we choose partners. Something is off, but we would rather hide behind our crazy beliefs than be vulnerable enough to face the truth.

Being able to understand that when you want to hide or be protective, you need to work harder at not buying into the false narrative our brains have created. Redirecting that energy and recognizing that it's more important to be vulnerable to the things that scare us, keeps us from falling back into the same old patterns. In becoming vulnerable, you must understand what your Knowns are but also be aware of your methods of self-protection. What do you do when you feel scared? Do you start to create a façade? Do you just hide from the world or not let anyone see the fractures? Whatever your method, you need to be aware.

Vulnerability is vital in ISC. If you can't be honest with yourself about what is really going on, you aren't being mindful. If you aren't being mindful, you can't do the work you need to do to move your life in a new direction that allows you to intuitively do self-care. How can you write an owner's manual if you don't thoroughly understand who you are…good, bad, and otherwise? This process is really about self-discovery and continuously finding ways to improve life, be at peace with yourself, and deal with the shit that holds you back from being who you want to be.

> Do you know when you are being protective of self?
> Do you hide behind a mask? When? Why?
> What opens you up to being susceptible?

What's On Your Self-Care List?

"Self-care is how you take your power back."

— Lalah Delia

Let's begin this chapter by defining self-care. Many people assume it's something selfish or indulgent; its neither. Self-care is a deliberate practice. It should be an intentional process of tending to your mind, body, and spirit. Practicing self-care enhances our health and wellbeing, helps manage stress and allows us to return to a level place where we feel content. Intuitive self-care differs from indulgence in that it restores order and peace of mind. For example, regularly eating a pint of Ben & Jerry's because you and your boyfriend have a strained relationship is not self-care because it's detrimental to your wellbeing, it will lead to more negative emotions. It will inherently add to your stress, whereas ISC will neutralize it. As you learn more about yourself, and what type of self-care works best, the process will become intuitive. You won't give it much thought; it will be a way of nurturing self.

I can't tell you how many times I've had a patient come in and assure me they are doing self-care regularly. When I ask them to tell me their list, it goes something like this. "Well, I exercise and eat

71

right and go hang out with my friends." When I ask how it's working for them, the response is, "that's why I'm here. I can't seem to relax, and I just don't think self-care works for me, I need something else."

I can't help but smile at this point because I know we need to work a bit harder at defining self-care. I like to tell them some of my favorite self-care items. My absolute number one self-care item is pressure washing. That's right; I love to pressure wash any and everything. When I tell this story, I probably sound like I think it's as good as sex, but for me, it's close. Once we all finish laughing at my love of pressure washing, I tell them that it's been years since I've had to use it for self-care. Why they ask? Because I haven't been that stressed out in years. I explain that pressure washing is the mack daddy of all self-care items for me. I also have a list of about 60-80 interventions, and they are quantified from light stress to heavy-duty stress relief.

So how do you make a list of self-care items? It begins by being keenly aware of self, knowing what you like, and what helps take you in a different direction. That direction, I can only describe as being in the moment, really sucked in. Imagine you are in your car and your favorite song comes on the radio. I'm talking old school, gonna rock out like you're having a concert for one. You know all the words and you even have some dance moves, or possibly an air guitar solo prepped and ready to roll. You are completely and totally sucked into this song, whatever it may be, and you are killing it with the performance of a lifetime. Until, of course, you look over and realize another driver is laughing their ass off at you. That is being in the moment, much like I was when I was rocking out to Bon Jovi! I use this example with everyone because I believe we have all experienced it. I mean, we all love music in some form or fashion.

Those few instances when you are completely immersed in a moment, and transported to another state of mind, that you completely forget everything going on around you. We've all had that moment at various times. Maybe you are just sitting on a beach somewhere when you get pulled into the sound of waves crashing, and the tranquility of the sunset unfolding before you. You are so mesmerized that you don't realize other people are also sharing this moment, what time it is, or even that you are getting cold. You are purely drawn into the beauty of the colors emerging as you watch the sun drop into the ocean.

Moments can be lengthy or short. A shorter moment can be as simple as looking into a loved one's eyes and truly seeing them. I do this with my children all the time. I glance over at them with their different facial expressions and admire how intent they are, or how happy. Regardless, I see them in their moment of life, and I appreciate what, and who, I see. This can be done with any person you know. Often, I remind myself to take snapshots of people, especially when I see joy or exhilaration on their faces. I mentally acknowledge those moments for what they are, and in turn, I feel their joy, then I carry that feeling with me, or recall that snapshot when I need a quick pick me up.

There are literally thousands, and thousands, of items we can have on our self-care list. They are all personal, there's no one size fits all list. Not everyone gets joy out of the same thing, and not everyone will have the same feeling about an experience. One of my people was adamant that she couldn't find more than four items to go on her list. Now, I can usually find items for people and help them rethink what they consider self-care. However, everything I offered her, she scrunched her nose and shook her head. I asked her to think about it and return with a few ideas. When she came back in, she smiled and told me about her most exciting find. She was doing clean-up in her classroom when she came across some old yarn that she had given her students to use for a project. She said she was about to throw it out but decided to see if she could salvage it. She spent hours and hours unknotting that yarn. As tedious a task as it was, the closer she got to reclaiming that tangled ball of yarn, she felt more and more relaxed. Once finished, she realized that she felt exhilaration, peace, and joy.

She found another item to add to her list, but it also gave her other ideas. When she spoke of that yarn, it reminded me of how I felt while pressure washing all those years ago. Like the biggest relief ever, control over the tension and stress, relaxation in a way that felt

74

empowering. Finding and adding items such as these is essential for you to practice self-care effectively.

Once you are able to identify plenty of components to add to your list, make sure you write them down. Yes, write-them-down. I always encourage my peeps to make an actual list of self-care items. The reason I want people to keep track of them is that when you are out of sorts, you won't remember what to do. You will be busy, lost in your stress, anxiety, panic, or just feeling overwhelmed. Without a list, you might revert to some old negative habits, like eating that pint of Ben & Jerry's. Having a real list in your phone, on your fridge, or stashed in your wallet will help you until you become completely versed in how to do self-care.

When you begin feeling out of sorts, you immediately go to the list and start doing what you need to do at the moment. You don't want to start with the mack daddy item, and honestly, for me, I don't always have access to a pressure washer. Start with something else and work your way through the list. This will help you determine the appropriate self-care item your stress correlates to. Another one of my favorite self-care items is to walk or do a few yoga poses or stretches. If that doesn't do the trick, I do a bit of meditation. Keep in mind, since I started using self-care this way, I can keep myself from getting too riled up. However, I also work hard at navigating my way through so that I avoid those things that cause me stress and strain. I had to figure this out, living in a constant state of stress isn't living; it's just existing.

This is my favorite portion of ISC. Why? Because it's the fun part of course. I learned years ago that I needed many items to help myself facilitate self-care. If we only had a couple of items on our list, we would exhaust them and most likely start to believe they weren't useful, causing us to give up. It's technically the intervention portion of ISC. It's where you learn to soothe yourself and give you what you need to navigate your way through the stressful world we live in.

You would think it was the most natural portion of ISC, but often the idea of self-care completely throws people off, either because they have never been taught how to do self-care, or they think it's selfish. To many people, self-care is exercise, manicures, pedicures, or massages. And it can be, but it is also so much more. Believe it or not, not everyone likes getting massages. The same goes for pedicures, manicures, and exercise. Some people like doing things such as coloring, painting, crafts, even laundry. Figuring out what works for you is the most crucial aspect of creating a list.

The reason we need self-care is that it's the way we regulate ourselves. ISC requires us to continually be in tune with ourselves and deciding what we need to remain in a level space. It always amazes me when my folks are completely unaware of what their level place is. Many of us are so used to riding the roller coaster of emotion that we have no idea what stable looks or feels like. Stability is exactly what ISC allows. No more wild ups and downs because you know how to manage yourself in a whole new way. One in which you feel positive and confident.

How do you know what to do, and when? It's mostly trial and error, but honestly, some common sense plays a part as well. If I get a bit stressed over getting everything packed and ready for my kids and myself to go on a family vacation, I won't break out the pressure washer. I might check my list then go outside and pull weeds in my garden. I may also decide to gather everyone, turn on some music, and play a game of Mexican Train (a current family favorite). Whatever I choose to do, it should be something that is equally proportionate to the stressor. Making a list in order of severity is a great idea, but they really are interchangeable for the most part. As you become more confident in your ability to understand what you need and when you need it, you will notice that it becomes an intuitive process.

Stress Level 1
- Listen to or sing music that sparks joy
- Text/call a friend
- Look at pics from a recent vacation or holiday

Stress level 2
- Go for a walk
- Grab a coffee or iced tea
- Watch a funny show or movie

Stress Level 3
- Do yoga poses or stretching
- Look at cute animal videos
- Get a change of scenery

Stress Level 4
- Meditate or read a book
- Sit in the sunlight
- Knock something off of your to-do-list

Stress Level 5
- Do laundry
- Play a game with the kids
- Cuddle with your partner or family member

Stress Level 6
- Get in the sauna or take a bubble bath
- Do a challenging workout
- Plan a date or vacation

Stress Level 7
- Go for a fun drive on a hilly road
- Go hiking in your favorite park
- Work on meal planning or organization

Stress Level 8
- Gardening
- Clean/organize something you've been avoiding
- Catch up on a favorite TV show/social media

Stress Level 9
- Go out into nature and actively absorb the goodness
- Go to a spiritual place for prayer, meditation, releasing of emotion
- Have good sex or intimacy with partner

Stress Level 10
- Break out the pressure washer
- Pull weeds
- Extreme exercise

Be sure to scale your stress level. I always pay very close attention to my body when I am trying to determine what intervention level I need. If I am about to lose my mind and scream or want to physically run away, that is probably a level 10. It goes down from there, but it is going to be different for everyone. A level 9 might be that I can feel my shoulders touching my ears, or as my massage therapist says, I am wearing my shoulders as earrings. I have probably been very stressed for quite some time. You should always do your best to be as mindful as possible and learn the signals your body sends you so that you don't get too revved up. Its easier to destress from a lower level than it is to have to go straight to your mack daddy self-care item. Either way, use the list of interventions appropriately. If you always go to the most powerful item, it won't be as effective. Save it for when you need it most.

Stress Cycle

Now that we have determined what some of the interventions can be. Let's look at where and when we would utilize them. Have you ever looked at or considered what your stress cycle looks like? Have you ever heard of a stress cycle? This might be one of the most important things I learned in graduate school. It's basically a way of mapping out how your body responds to stress. I usually draw a big circle on a page and then start looking for responses to stress that

79

the person I'm working with describes. We plot them out like we are creating a timeline of events leading up to the moment when they can no longer handle their stress.

Starting at the top, you try to remember what the earliest signs and signals are that you experience. It will usually be something relatively benign like maybe you feel the urge to move around or change positions. The next signal might be that you notice your hands start to sweat. Followed by something a bit more noticeable like your shoulders getting tight or another part of your body tensing up. Next, it might progress into your stomach feeling queasy or upset, escalating into a tight or pressure like feeling in your chest. As the symptoms continue to escalate, you will notice that they heighten to a place where none of us want to go. Sadly, it will eventually happen unless we stop the cycle with an intervention of some sort. The earlier we utilize the intervention, the better the outcome we get. This is the entire purpose of mapping the stress cycle. If we can identify these signals within ourselves and understand how we react, we'll also know how to fix it.

STRESS CYCLE

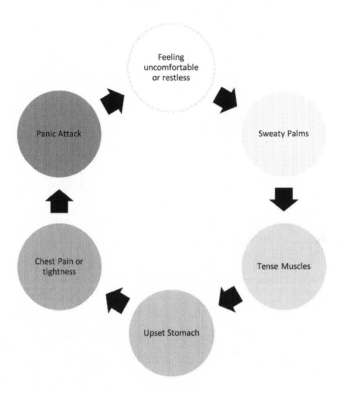

After we have spent time learning our cycle, we can then use our list of self-care items to redirect if necessary. I always have my people create their stress cycle with a list of interventions, or self-care items, on the side or back of the same document. That way, when they first start this process, they can find direct correlations between their level of stress and the corresponding intervention. One without the other is useless.

Your list needs to consist of positive self-care items. I've had people come into my office with negative items on their list. Eating, drinking, and doing anything you want is not self-care. In fact, overdoing anything is not self-care at all. Some people think using alcohol, drugs, sex, or anything else indulgent is a way of taking care of themselves when they feel anxious or stressed. This couldn't be further from the truth. I ask that you consider what effects your self-care routine has on you. If you commonly need to drink a few beers or cocktails after work to destress, then you may have a problem. I remember a colleague who shared that she went home every day and drank a six-pack. She did this for about a year before she realized that she was misusing alcohol; this was not self-care, nor was it a good coping mechanism. Since she was a therapist, she was able to look at her behavior and gradually began replacing her drinking with something more healthy over time. She chose bike riding as a way to do self-care and help her stop progressively using alcohol. She expanded into other activities and successfully gave up the beer.

Remember that moderation is the goal, but do consider what you are utilizing. Again, too much of anything isn't a good idea. If you have an addiction or know you may have a problem, then it should not be considered self-care. We want to create a list that is positive and holistic. That is, it should be good for the mind, body, and spirit. Everyone will have different items on their list. Don't get caught up in what someone else does. Just because you don't like pressure washing means nothing, it's not for everyone. Do what feels good to you, as long as it's not harmful to self or others.

In addition to positive and negative aspects of self-care, there are varying areas of life that need to be addressed. Each area needs its own focus. What I use for personal self-care isn't exactly what I would do for work-related stress. Even relationship self-care is going to require something somewhat different. I encourage everyone to make various lists for the different areas of our lives. Once you determine what you need to do for yourself regularly, it will be something you can't live without. You will get so good at it you won't give it a second thought. However, you have to practice and learn all aspects of self-care, mindfulness, and self-awareness.

What symptoms are on your stress cycle?
Which interventions work best?

What Is Your Energy Signature?

"Energy doesn't communicate in English, French, Chinese, or Swahili, but it does speak clearly."

— Elaine Seiler

What on earth is an energy signature, you might ask? It's the way you address or greet the world! Sound important? It is, your energy signature attracts or repels people every moment of the day. Are you aware of what your's say about you?

Let's talk about the energy part first. You've heard this term before. I use it frequently, mostly because I am so much more aware of how it affects us daily, but I am also still learning to fine-tune the intuitive and innate skill I've always had but didn't pay close enough attention to. Sometimes when I comment on energy, I get a raised eyebrow or puzzled look, but they know what I mean. Turns out, energy has many different names; some people refer to it as a vibe, mood, tone, gut feeling, emotional energy, or life force. Whatever you call it, we've all experienced it. Some people feel great to be around, they lighten our moods and make us feel safe, while other people drain us and make us want to vacate immediately. Psychologists refer to it as "social evaluation" which has been studied in preverbal children as young as five months old as well as in animals. Both babies and animals showed significant capabilities in determining negative and positive energy. Although they also both responded most heavily to negative energy. Shocking, right? Scientists have discovered it to be a leftover evolutionary process that helps both humans and animals determine when danger is imminent but is also considered necessary for navigating the social world (Hamilton et al., 2007). Basically, we are born with the ability to sense friend or foe.

Some of the ways in which we tune into energy are through a person's eyes, overall physical presence, physical contact, tone, and or volume of voice and capacity for empathy. You've heard the phrase, "the eyes are the window into the soul." It's true, look into a happy babies' eyes, or in the eyes of someone who loves you, and you can feel their intensity and zest. The same goes for a smile or laughter. When I see people smiling and laughing, I feel like everything is right for them in their world, it makes me feel good that they feel good. The same goes for empathic people. The difference between a person who is open and capable of sharing feelings and someone who is guarded is noticeable. I know who I want to be around, do you? Whatever the measure, our senses evolved to include this fantastic ability, yet we often forget about reflecting on what type of energy we are giving off. That's because we are used to feeling a certain way, or we just aren't in touch with ourselves. I personally think this step to being intuitive is one of the most difficult to master. However, as with all of the ideas that I am bringing to you, I think it is worth the effort and certainly something you can continue to work on for the rest of your life. This is the signature part. Are you aware of your energy signature?

Over the years, I've learned the energy people put out there doesn't always match what they feel, say, or do. I get people in my office all the time that try desperately to make things seem one way, but the energy or vibe I get from them doesn't sync at all with what they are saying. In years past, I wasn't as good at asking about the inconsistency, but I know I could feel it. Now, I call it like I see it. If people are nervous or anxious, I offer to go walk outside during our session or go out into the memorial garden in an effort to get their energy to soften. When someone comes in, and I can feel their anger or agitation, I always acknowledge it because I know it happens to be a sore spot for me. Remember those Knowns? Well, anger and agitation can trigger emotions for me, so I have to work at self-care while still being available for my person. Can you imagine if I weren't aware of this? I might come off as being aloof, insensitive, or a complete bitch. However, once I point it out, people generally try to self-regulate, but if it's not something they can readily do on their own, I have a few tricks up my sleeve. I can't imagine carrying all that anger or agitation around with me. That sounds awful. So, utilizing my Spidey senses allows me to do my job better while also being aware of my own needs.

How do you tune in to your own energy? This task isn't as easy as you might think. To be able to tune in to self, we need to do a self-assessment on a regular basis. Much like taking your temperature, but this is more like doing a system check throughout the day. Ask yourself how you feel at the moment, and does your physical expression match your internal emotion? If you aren't sure what kind of energy you are putting off, ask someone close to you. I have found that we aren't always aware of how we present to others, especially when we are busy or a lot is going on around us. Listen to your inner voice, are your thoughts positive, do you feel clear-headed, or are your thoughts racing? Are you paying attention to how your body feels? Do your muscles feel relaxed, are you breathing normally, do you feel good in your own skin? These and many other questions can be asked during a system check. It doesn't have to take long, and it should be tailored to fit you and how you respond to the world. Once you do it regularly, it will become second nature.

Energy is a combination of a person's physical energy, governing thoughts, mindset, perception of the world around them, and their past. It can be affected by many factors, but generally, we aren't taught to be mindful of it. It took me many years to understand what energy was. We have all experienced it, but it's difficult to describe. I had to sit with hundreds of people to be able to identify energy. This could be because I was caught up in my own shit for too long and unable to tune in. I've actually gotten quite good identifying others energy, so much so that I feel my body respond if someone is too anxious or angry. It's a valuable tool for me at this point. However, recognizing someone else's energy versus being conscious of your own, is an entirely different story.

The idea of adding awareness of your own energy came to mind when my husband and I were on vacation. We were in beautiful Sedona, Arizona, celebrating our second anniversary. My husband likes to be very active during our vacations, so we usually have our days planned out. I am always aware of our itinerary, but there was one day that he had planned a surprise for me. It was identified as our "relaxation day."

Keep in mind that my husband and I have different ideas about relaxation. He's always taking care of business and absolutely ahead of whatever is happening in our lives. Planning is self-care for him. He doesn't really get stressed about things because as he plans life, he always plans for self-care, which is usually being active in some form. So, hearing we had a relaxation day was a tiny bit concerning to me. We also hadn't been able to be as active as we usually would be due to weather conditions. I was a little concerned about how he was feeling and if he was enjoying himself.

It was mid-week, so I thought I'd do a load of laundry before my surprise. The laundry idea didn't go quite as planned. First, the machines were small, so I needed to split the load, which meant I had to go back to our casita to get more detergent. When I returned, I noticed that the soap wasn't dissolving, so I had to go back again to get a different type, then I realized I was cutting it close on time because I needed to rewash everything. I was stressed out because my day wasn't going smoothly, and I didn't know what to expect from my surprise.

To add to the fun, my wonderful husband walked in and asked if he could go change the clothes over. Of course, I said no, because he wouldn't know what went in the dryer and what should be air-dried. I was trying to shower and get ready because time was ticking for my surprise. I needed to be ready, have the laundry complete, and be in a good place. Instead, I was feeling stressed, and as a result, the energy I was giving off looked a lot like anger. My poor husband thought I was angry with him.

I wasn't angry at all, I was stressed. It's quite common for stress to look like anger to the people around you. This is why it's essential to be aware of your energy signature. Thomas was aware. He even asked if I was angry, and I scoffed at him saying, "why would I be angry, we are on vacation, and I have a surprise!" Kind of snarky, huh? Not my finest moment.

I did apologize for my behavior and let him know I was stressed and not angry. He was wonderful as usual and offered to tell me the surprise. I declined and realized I needed to take my temperature. I needed to find a way to destress quickly. Now that I was being more self-aware, I tried to calm my energy. I asked if we could stop for a latte before the surprise and maybe afterward if we could go to Amitabha Stupa Peace Park. Although I had never been to a place like it, I thought it might have good energy and allow me to redirect myself. Turns out, it was exactly what I needed. I felt my energy shift as we walked along the paths and took time for a bit of meditation.

The surprise my husband had planned was a spa day, with our first couple's massage. We had access to a pool, soaking tub, steam shower, sauna, chocolates, and champagne. It was an incredible afternoon, to say the least. Yes, I have a fantastic partner who makes me want to be a better person. As I considered the day, I realized it was important for me to do a better job of being aware of myself and my energy. Did I really want to be perceived as an angry bitch who lives an incredible life? NO! I want to live my best life and mirror the emotional energy that I'm experiencing. I want to be positive in my actions and put positive energy out into the world. Damn it!

Another aspect of your energy signature is facial expressions. What is your face doing? Are you smiling? If you are genuinely smiling, you are showing the world how you feel. I'm not talking about the fake smile some people wear plastered on their faces. I'm talking about a genuinely happy smile, a smile that goes all the way to your eyes. Your face gives information to the world, and it's important to be aware of what it is. I'm not saying we should always be smiling, but we should always be conscious of our energy. Then we have some control over how we are perceived.

Anne

One of my peeps, Anne, told me a story about how she was received by her parents during a recent trip to visit them for the weekend. For years she and her parents had difficulties communicating and often felt frustrated with each other because of it. Upon arrival, her parents immediately felt as if something was wrong with her and went on the defensive. She asked me why people always assumed she was mad when really if they knew her, they would understand that she was really just a deep thinker, and they shouldn't get upset by her being lost in her head. I asked her if it was problematic, and she acknowledged that her husband and kids always assumed she was mad too. She hadn't realized that her being lost in thought, looked a lot like someone who was upset.

Like Anne, we all have to recognize how we are perceived by others. If we are not happy, or we are having a bad day, what do others feel from us? It's not that we can't have a bad day or a rough patch, but if we are really evaluating ourselves and being mindful, we should then notice the discrepancy between what we feel and the energy we are giving off. It is another tool to help us understand how best to take care of ourselves. If my outside doesn't match the inside, what's going on? What do I need to do to feel centered and at peace?

Self-care and mindfulness are great ways to be centered and find peace. I won't lie about it; it takes time and effort to create a place where you can be in a state of true calm. Especially if you have experienced trauma and struggled through life. However, it can be done. You can achieve it with time and effort dedicated to understanding self. We often forget that we do get to choose what kind of life we live. We have to choose to be the best version of ourselves, and that includes learning how to take care of self.

So, what do we do differently? We have gotten very comfortable picking up on cues and clues from others and what kind of vibes they are giving off. However, we aren't stopping to listen to our inner dialogue and consider how we are feeling. Ask yourself, how is my mood and energy affecting others? Pay attention to how others act when they are around you. Does the vibe get weird when you enter the room? People often mimic the energy they pick up on. That, or they will try to change negative energy, like anger or anxiety by cracking a joke, or tiptoeing around a person. Being aware of self and how others perceive us is quite palpable if we are actively engaged in the practice of mindfulness.

Anne has done the work and is actively paying attention to how she presents. She doesn't always have a smile on her face, but she is aware of how she is feeling. She had a conversation with her kids about what it means when Mom is "in her head" and how to ask her if she is good or having a bad day. She noticed that the household is happier because they aren't always trying to figure out if Anne is in a bad mood. She also actively tries to smile when she is happy. Anne noticed that she was in a rut and allowed her past and depression to keep her from smiling. She was always scared the other shoe was going to drop. By understanding how to take good care of herself and being aware, she can focus on the good around her.

Positivity is something we should all work toward, but we get stuck. Gratitude is a wonderful way to redirect ourselves. Whether we have had a tough life or not, recognizing when things are good, and being grateful for those things, helps us be in a positive mindset. Also, consciously choosing to be kind, compassionate, and loving, helps us feel as if we are putting goodness out into the world because we are. Seriously, who wants to be negative, it takes too much energy. Besides, if I can respond with love and kindness, it usually comes back to me. If it doesn't, I always tell myself that I have planted a seed of goodness, or at least stopped the negativity for someone so that they might have a better day.

Other ways that I find positivity and good energy is by creating joy in my life. If I search for peace and joy in my life daily, then I am for sure living my best life. When we actively seek goodness, we are going to be happier. Taking time to enjoy our lives, and do things that make us happy, is imperative when doing self-care and maintaining positive energy. We have to monitor our thoughts to keep the negative thoughts from overtaking us, and there is no better way of doing that than being completely present. As discussed previously, being present and totally in the moment allows us to stop those negative, stressful, anxiety-provoking habits. If we anticipate negative things will happen, then we are setting ourselves up for that negativity to influence our energy.

Paying attention to your energy is a great way to find happiness and live a calm, peaceful life. Once you have accomplished the energy component of ISC, you are well on your way to living your best life and influencing others around you. It is like unwrapping more of life's presents.

Have you encountered people with negative energy signatures?
What vibe do you give off?
If you meet someone with great energy, what do you notice most?

Who Do You Want To Be?

"Find out who you are and do it on purpose."

— Dolly Parton

You might be curious about this question because most people think they have a good idea of who they are, but if we are going to restructure our lives through the use of mindfulness and self-care, then it seems reasonable to ask the question. Through the awareness of ISC, you will discover some crucial truths about self, while also gaining an advantage and control that most people only wish they possessed. You will feel different, and you will react to the world around you differently. So much so that you will be able to achieve an awakening of sorts. In fact, you will be able to redirect your energy toward becoming who you want to be instead of always fighting the things that have shaped you and held you back as a person. Most of us believe we are who we are without giving any thought to the idea that we are all truly a work in progress and on our own journeys. We are who we decide to be, but only if we are self-aware enough to maintain it and not allow our past to direct us. Think about it, if we aren't resolving old belief systems and untangling our crap, aren't we really just perpetuating it? Why would we want to continue doing that?

Most of the time, when I work with people and ask the important question about who they want to be, I get a puzzled look. Not because its an odd question, but most people don't realize how impactful their knowns and beliefs have been in molding them. Sometimes, people cry in response to this question. The tears represent healing and growth, and I have to remind them that this is a gift they are giving themselves. It's what I consider to be the reward for doing the hard work required for the creation of true inner peace. Getting a person to this point is what I absolutely love about my job. Seeing change is incredible, but watching a person get to a place of deep understanding of self, is beyond words for me. It's almost a spiritual experience that I get to share with a person, and it's profoundly satisfying to be there to see.

When people are stumped by the question about who they want to be, it's important to remind them that after they have mastered ISC, the mindfulness and self-care will help them develop new skills and shift from those unhelpful Knowns and false beliefs. Reframing your perspective on who you are is part of the process of becoming mindful. Social psychologists call it cognitive or positive re-appraisal. Positive re-appraisal is an adaptive process in which stressful events are reframed as being "benign, valuable, or beneficial" (Garland, 2009). Think about it, if we are always self-reflective and give value to our thoughts, then we react differently. We are no longer frightened by the old crap that has followed us around because we stop and think about how we want to respond. When I suggest doing this, the first question that follows is what if it takes a while for me to formulate an answer? I say, so what?! Maybe at first, you won't be quick with your responses, but why do you need to be? Isn't a well thought out response worth waiting for? As you get used to being mindful and redirecting yourself, responses will come more quickly, especially as you create new neuropathways.

So why ask this question that obviously poses such perplexity? Because if we do the work to become self-aware and understand what and how created beliefs or Knowns have impacted us, we also understand that they are collectively no longer needed. Considering that our worldview is now different because we no longer hold the same value system, then it doesn't stand to reason that we need these ideologies anymore. When you upgraded to a smartphone, did you still carry around your old flip phone? These old tool belts won't be helpful to you moving forward, and therefore a new tool belt must be created. So the question then becomes, what are you left with? Who are you at this point? This is where the question becomes increasingly important. Who do you want to be? The old crap holding you back is no longer relevant, so now what? Do you want to operate from a level of growth and self-awareness? Then you must navigate a new path.

Chaps

So what kind of new tool belt do you need? That is an interesting question, to say the least. It will keep changing as you continue being mindful and utilizing self-care as a way of life. I have a joke in my office about old worn-out tool belts. I liken them to a pair of super comfy jeans that fit like a glove. You know the ones I'm talking about, they aren't perfect anymore, they may have a few holes or stains, but they feel so good to slide into. The problem is they keep getting holes and start to look like a pair of chaps. Now, I'm confident there is a time and place for chaps, but for most of us, they aren't a good look. Seriously, all the important parts are no longer covered. My people always laugh at this metaphor, but it's accurate. Plus, it's also a great way to create change. By creating a strongly negative view of those chaps, I'll be less likely to use them. Especially if I am aware that by using my old tool belt, I am actively putting on a pair of chaps, then I'm going to reconsider. It's not the look I'm going for. I mean, who wants to show their ass?

If any of the things you held as true change, for whatever reason, doesn't that change how you see and operate within the world? If you dismantle those beliefs and knowns, then who are you? The old code to life that you once held tightly, no longer seems appropriate or useful. You need a new tool belt filled with tools and techniques to handle yourself in the world. To create your new tool belt, it's going to be essential to know yourself well. Yes, you need to be aware of your Knowns and beliefs but also a few key points about how you operate. Are you an introvert or an extrovert? Why is this important? Introverts need downtime to re-energize while extroverts get re-energized by people. If I need to know how best to take care of myself, I need to know when and how to charge the batteries. Recharging is essential to us as humans. No one I know can survive long, much less be on top of their game, without recharging. You also need to ask yourself what changes need to be made, and are they plausible?

If you read self-help books, you will get a consistent message about becoming the person you most want to be. I love this idea and often discuss it with my patients. Asking them who they want to be helps people identify what it is that they want or need to change. However, this is also difficult for many to completely understand because they often come into my office knowing what is wrong, but they have no idea what they really want for themselves.

A vital part of asking yourself who you want to be is based on your experiences. I've read many incredibly motivating books, but they suggest you simply get over the negative things that you've felt or dealt with within your lifetime. I would love nothing more than to believe that we could just forget about all the bad things that have influenced our make up. The problem with that philosophy is that the brain doesn't work like a computer that we can just delete info from. In reality, even computers maintain the information, and a good forensic IT person can recover most, if not all info from a computer.

Our brains work in a wonderful way. We can decide we will not get hung up on some aspect of our lives, and we can actually do a great job of outrunning our emotions. One of my pet peeves is that often people try to go over, under, or around emotions without realizing it will catch up to us at some point. I have spent enough time with patients on a clinical level to see this happen to everyone that tries. You can run, but you can't hide, as the saying goes. Facing emotions is difficult for many of us. One of my favorite sayings in the psychoeducation world is: Feelings aren't facts. However, they sure can feel that way. Unless, of course, you are able to utilize mindfulness and self-care in a manner that allows you to no longer feel overwhelmed by feelings and emotions. Would that change who you are as a person?

Let's say we actually look at our life experiences differently. Instead of trying just to let things go, what if we saw them as life lessons and ways in which we became who we are. The difference in what I am suggesting here is to distinguish between what you have learned and need to catalog, and deciding what needs to be recognized as important but not allowed to have undue influence.

For instance, let's say you have not had great experiences with dating. You could identify this as what you will be saddled with for the rest of your life. "I just can't meet a good partner, they are all married or gay!" this is something you are telling yourself, not necessarily your truth. If we dig into this statement and understand where it originated, we might find that you had a bad relationship in high school and another in college. Why were they so bad? Well, you may have had a negative self-image and dated the only person that you thought you were worthy of dating. Maybe you didn't think the good-looking person you had a serious crush on would ever look at you because you had acne, and lord forbid anyone ever have acne.

These are false truths we have told ourselves. When we are telling ourselves these false truths, we begin to believe them. So, forever, acne is the reason we can't pursue more attractive people, which turns into, I am not worthy of dating someone I'm really attracted to, which turns into, I should just go out with this person who isn't that nice because, well, he doesn't seem to mind that I have a pimple or two on my face. Once we lower our standards and continue to believe these ideas we have about ourselves, then we begin living our lives based on this crap we have made up.

My response to this is to question everything about yourself. Why the hell did you come up with such a lame idea to begin with? Now keep in mind we make bad decisions and come up with the biggest loads of horse manure when we are young, but honestly, I've seen grown adults do it or maintain the lies for years and years. So much so that it has become their truth.

How do we differentiate between lies or falsehoods and reality? We work on our knowns and beliefs. Understanding our knowns and really understanding self is the most imperative portion of becoming intuitive about self-care. The more we understand how we think, where our crap comes from, why we created some of these ideas, to begin with, or even how we came to believe various things, we can then begin to unravel these stories and see them for what they are, not real!

Why would we need to be able to identify all of these falsehoods before we begin making changes? Because we need to know where the crap came from so that we can declutter. Professional organizers encourage us to go through our belongings and decide what we need to keep and what should be tossed. It's important to determine what is necessary, what is useful, and what brings us joy. Now, often people get stuck in the weeds while doing this, but if you really are accountable and you are completely honest with yourself, you realize that hanging on to a macaroni art project from your child from eight years ago is useless even if it brings happiness to you for a moment. Take a picture and allow yourself to be less encumbered by things. Well, what if we did that with some of our experiences or feelings. What if we really understood which things made us who we are and how they affected us. Once we know this, we can easily begin the process of deciding what needs to be thrown out, what needs to be given away, and neatly fold and organize what we deem worthy.

What does this have to do with determining who you want to be? That part is quite easy. Just like any show we watch on TV about Hoarders or organizing, there is a huge mess, and you can't really distinguish what is what. I mean, yes, there is a house, it's in a town, on a street, there are walls and flooring, and maybe you can see the brick on the outside. However, beyond that, it's just a holding station for a bunch of crap. Is that how you want to walk through life?

I meet people like this all the time. There is useless crap so piled up, they can't determine what is what for themselves. They may have an education or great career, they are working, they have friends and family, they have emotions and feelings, they have all the stuff they are supposed to have, but they feel overwhelmed because they don't know what to do with all of the emotional baggage that they are hauling around everywhere they go. They have no idea what life would look like if they tidied up their brains, determined what they actually wanted out of life, and began operating from the standpoint of knowing who they are instead of just pretending.

It's the emotional baggage and old tales we keep telling ourselves, or that our brains keep replaying over and over like a worn-out CD. We take these ideas on as truth and hold on to them like they are gospel. These ideas can be anything from a severe trauma that happened to some idea you created on your own as a child learning lessons in this challenging world.

To create our authentic selves or know who we really want to be, we have to declutter. We need to understand where we came from to be able to move forward. Knowing how we react and what got us to these points in our lives allows us to begin cleaning the rooms out one by one and begin to see what life really looks like. We can start to know what we really want out of life, we can see our futures with clarity because we have done the work to organize what we need to keep and then we get to start allowing ourselves to live within our truth. Once we are unclouded and unburdened by the lies we have created and with the realization of how some hang-ups were developed. We are then capable of knowing ourselves to the point that we can now navigate around these ideas. We can simply decide if we want to react based on something that happened to us in our past or if we want to respond differently.

This is differentiation at its finest. Instead of differentiating with our families, we can differentiate from our old selves. Moving away from the things we created in our minds that make us who we are.

Keeping what works for ourselves and understanding how negative things have affected us and shaped us as human beings.

The differentiation process is a significant one. Once we differentiate, we can then begin creating a manual for self with determinations like, this is who I am, this is how I react to various stimuli, I do best in this particular setting, I don't do well in that setting. All of which allows you to navigate through life with more intent. You know what to do, when to do it, how to take care of yourself. You are essentially a machine with a GPS and an internal monitoring system with readjustment technology. Sounds pretty good, right?

The final portion of this quest to become an evolved human is truly about being okay with who you are, flaws and all. Can you be happy with yourself and the life you have lived even if it isn't, or hasn't been, perfect? Are you working toward being the person you want to be? How conscious are you of the person you are constructing through self-awareness?

All of those questions matter because you get the chance to decide every day who you want to be. I think it's a question we ask ourselves if we are fully aware of self. Some of the questions are large, and some are small, but undoubtedly they are important in helping us define who we are as people. We are a culmination of decisions we make throughout the day. However, once you overcome the influences of your past, you can then start making better decisions for yourself. You will be unfettered, with a vision in mind.

Asking yourself who you want to be often leads people down a curious road. As I mentioned earlier, it's a scary and curious question so, I always suggest we consider the people we admire most. Ask yourself why you admire them and what you can do to be more like them. Make a list of several people while being sure you understand precisely why you admire them. Don't look for people who have more than you do, look at their traits, values, and overall character. Once you do this, set goals for yourself to make changes. You don't have to do it all at once, but over time you can achieve these changes. Becoming who you want to be is an amazing gift. It's like feeling great in your own skin and moving through the world with purpose.

Do you recognize any old beliefs that need to be challenged?
Do you know who you want to be?
Are you actively making changes toward growth as a human? If so, what changes have you made?

Creating An Owner's Manual

"Peace is a daily, a weekly, a monthly process, gradually changing opinions, slowly eroding old barriers, quietly building new structures."

—John F. Kennedy

Now that you have learned the different parts of ISC, you are ready to create an Owner's Manual. That's right, you know how to utilize all of the controls, bells, and whistles to maintain self. You will always be updating and forever upgrading because we never get to stop improving. Living an ISC lifestyle will invariably mean you are growing as a human.

There are several steps to creating your owner's manual; I have broken them down so that it's a bit easier when you begin this process. Don't worry, it gets more natural, and I promise it becomes an instinctual/intuitive process. Combining all of the elements of ISC allows us to create an owner's manual in four steps.

Dissect and Evaluate

Roots & Origins

Self Care & Redirection

Change

Dissect & Evaluate

The first steps begin with becoming mindful of your surroundings. We dissect and evaluate by looking around and paying close attention to how we react to things. This is why understanding your "Knowns" and "beliefs" is important. Ask yourself how you feel. What is your energy like around certain people and situations? Do you get anxious or feel stressed? What are the symptoms and signs of your anxiety/stress? Do you have strong beliefs that direct behavior? Are you feeling tense? Are you wearing your shoulders like earrings? Is an experience nagging at you or causing you to be closed off? Are you feeling frightened, depressed, anxious, or overwhelmed about various "Knowns" that have impacted you as a person? When do these things come up? What is happening around you, and how does it make you feel? Does being in a certain area of town make you uncomfortable? This is what being mindful means. All of these questions and more need to be evaluated so that you can craft a plan of attack. If we know how we operate, then we know where our glitches are.

Roots & Origins

Once you have figured out when you are feeling off, what belief systems are problematic, and what "Knowns" are regularly creeping up and causing issues, we can begin to understand why. As discussed in chapter three, we look at roots and origins. If we know where our glitches are coming from, we can take a step back and ask ourselves if we still want to react in the same way. We can also use the knowledge to soothe ourselves.

If, for example, you get nervous when you travel across bridges, you can ask yourself where that emotion originated, and then realize you saw an awful movie when you were a kid depicting a bridge collapse, or maybe you have a fear of heights that comes from nearly falling off a cliff while hiking with your family. Either way, you now understand where it comes from. Make sure you analyze the situation thoroughly. There may be several compounding components that are contributing.

Remember, the origin could come from anywhere. You may have been taught things as a child, or even as an adult that are based on belief systems. Families are full of these beliefs, and we should carefully assess what works for the lives we want to live versus what other people have influenced you to believe to be true. If your FOO believes that there is only one acceptable religion, then your desire to explore other faiths might feel like it is wrong, or you will be criticized for it.

Beliefs can also stem from a class you took or from a book you read or even a TV show you watched. Challenge these ideas and make sure they accurately depict who you want to be and aren't things that have been impressed upon you. Do these beliefs support who you want to be as a person?

Sometimes the roots come from trauma. If they are traumatic, have you done the work to unpack it all and expand it so that they are less triggering? Do you need help or support in doing that? Be aware of what you need and seek help. I've met folks who were totally unaware of the impact a moment in their past was inflicting upon them. Until we understand ourselves on a deeper level, we can't redirect and do self-care properly.

Self Care & Redirection

Once we figure out what things are affecting us, when they are impacting us, and where they originate from, we get to redirect ourselves using self-care. This step gets confused with being selfish, but it's not selfish at all. It's about understanding yourself and knowing what you need, why you need it, and how to do it. If your tire needed air and the indicator light came on, would you stop to put air in the tire? Is that considered selfish of the tire? You don't have time to stop at the moment, but if you put it off, what could happen? Well, you might get a flat tire soon, or it could be a slow leak. Either way, you best figure it out because nobody has time for a blowout. True self-care is about being so aware of yourself that you feel things as they happen, much like a real-time indication system.

Having awareness allows us to redirect ourselves and make better choices. In chapter 9, we look at self-care and create lists of things we can do for ourselves. Utilize the list so that you can self-correct. Do not get stuck repeating the same stuff over and over, expecting a different outcome. It won't happen. You get to find ways that make life easier in addition to really knowing who you are as a person.

If you know what you need when you need it, you will find peace. Self-care should be a way of life. It should be in real-time and not put off for another day or saved for next month when you go on vacation. Doing even small things for yourself, as the stresses and strains of everyday life come up, is essential. Stopping to do some of the lower level stress items discussed in chapter four, is a great way to be present and maintain clarity so that you are less stressed throughout the day.

Operating in a neutral stance is the goal. Waiting until you are overwhelmed makes getting back to neutral more difficult. When you feel off, ask yourself what you need to fix it as it's happening. That's what self-care is. Its also about knowing what it takes to remedy the situation.

Remember that self-care needs to be positive. Anything negative or that causes harm to self or others is not going to be considered self-care. Having a shot of whiskey every night before bed is not a good idea. I've met people who have become full-on alcoholics after doing this for weeks or months. It's not intentional, it just becomes an easy fix, and eventually, you need a couple of shots, and then you start drinking throughout the day. Keep the self-care positive. Too much of anything isn't good, which is why we create a list of many different self-care items. That way, you have lots to choose from, and you create a rather large tool belt. I ask my peeps to develop an arsenal because you never know when you will have to get super crafty. One person told me about being stuck in a vehicle with her kids and in-laws on a long trip, and she was about to scream. She popped in her earbuds and created a song list for vacation, one of which she named "Stuck in the van with crazy." It made her giggle, which lowered her stress level and redirected her thoughts immediately. Another person told me about a mantra she recites when she needs it. She made it up to follow a cute, well-known jingle that allows her to revise it with new words and expletives to fit the situation. Find what soothes you and brings you peace without causing harm.

Change

Change is a scary thing to do. Ask anyone who has made a big move in life, and they will concur. We get so used to being comfortable that we stay in situations that aren't good for us.

This is known as the homeostasis effect. Even if it's terrible, it's our normal.

I've learned as a therapist that people want change but are rarely willing to give up the comfort of what they know. Hearing many reasons or excuses, why change is impossible is pretty common in my profession. This is often where people get stuck, but if they can muster up the gumption to make even the smallest change and they get a positive outcome, look out world more change is on the horizon.

In chapter 8, we discuss who you want to be. This step is incredibly important to even be able to imagine change. Without knowing what you want, you certainly can't go out and get it. I always use the analogy of buying a car with this step. If you want a new car, you have given some thought to what kind you want. Do you want a compact car, a sedan, an SUV, or a truck? What color? How much money do you want to spend? All of these questions lead you to go out and to get what you want. You also have to know what fits best in your life. Obviously, you don't need a two-seater sports car if you have four kids to cart around. You also don't want to buy a vehicle you can't afford. You must know precisely what you want, or you will end up getting something that isn't useful and brings no joy.

Understanding who you want to be requires you to ask similar questions. Do your belief systems allow you to be who you want to be? Do past traumas affect you or keep you from being that person? Without knowing who you are and looking deeply at how you were formed as a person with all of your experiences, you can't be who you want to be. What's more, you won't know what you need to move in a different direction. Having this information allows you to be better informed to make better decisions for self.

Knowing how change works for you is important to know as well. Often, we plan on making changes and get discouraged when it doesn't work out as we had hoped. Ever make a New Year's resolution only to slack off in a few weeks? Most of us have done this and realize how bad it makes us feel. When someone repeatedly falls short, they create a belief system that they are not capable of making change and are less likely to try.

You wouldn't believe the excuses I have heard people come up with to avoid change or potentially failing again at something else. Because of this, I encourage my peeps to evaluate when they have been successful in making changes, even small or insignificant ones. There is a formula to it, what works for you? Likewise, is the goal realistic? What are the steps? How will you track it? Will you focus on progress or only concentrate on perfection? What environment do you need to be most successful? What gets you stuck? What helps keep you motivated? All of these questions will help you find the best course of action when attempting to apply change that is considered second order. Second-order change is transformational because it involves seeing the world completely different and ultimately creates permanent or lasting change.

Once we have accomplished the lofty goal of understanding ourselves and knowing what we want, we can create change more easily. In fact, you should begin to feel that tug of desire toward calm after looking within. You will feel different, as if you see everything more clearly, with more compassion and understanding of how life has influenced you. You will be in more control of the change you look for because you can see how the pieces fit. Change will become necessary, and once you get a taste of it, you will do whatever it takes to stay in this desired place of calm and purpose.

Putting it all together

This is the best part of creating your owner's manual. Take all of the things you have learned and begin creating a guide. I suggest you utilize the questions throughout the book to get a good start on knowing what you need to discover about self. I always tell my people it's just like a car's owner manual. If you need to know what kind of oil to put in your new vehicle, you look in the manual to find out what you need to know. Just like your Owner's Manual for Self, you will keep track of what your issues are and know what to do, or at the very least, you will know where to begin to soothe yourself and redirect.

A personal owner's manual allows us to compile information about ourselves. It's going to be an ever-changing guide to who you are as you age and learn more about yourself. You can imagine that you won't be the same person at 45 that you were at 25. At least, I hope you aren't. I know for sure I am a completely different person than I was even ten years ago. It's fun to see how you change and what you realize about yourself as you go on this journey of self-discovery. Knowing what to do and when to do it makes perfect sense for being able to navigate life better. You have to really learn your habits, check your thoughts, take your temperature, and be very aware of self. This will help you reconfigure how your brain processes the crap you are carrying around.

The self-care portion is what you will actively do when you realize that you are stressed, anxious, depressed, frustrated, etc. Those feelings are outward responses to internalized emotions. What exactly is causing these emotions to flare up? What do you need to do about them? What has helped in the past? Get creative about making a list with as much self-care as you can. You could have 50-100 items that are positive interventions if you keep working at it. Grasping what works best for each Known is going to give you the influence to redirect your thoughts and potentially create new neuropathways. Over time, you will notice the old crap isn't as bothersome because you have those new neuropathways. It takes time, but it happens.

After doing all of this work, you will be able to progressively redirect your thoughts, feelings, and emotions so that you have more command of self. You will notice a tremendous calm and peace take over because your negative experiences are no longer leading you in life. All the trauma, strain, and struggle doesn't have to be in control. You get to live life again on your terms.

By doing all of the work to understand what keeps us from moving forward with the life we want, we move into challenging ourselves even further. We do this by way of being vulnerable. We have to face what scares us. We have to learn how to take care of ourselves by assessing whether or not we are susceptible to the old crap we just learned about ourselves. In doing so, we are on our way to learning self-care and ultimately self-love.

Every moment requires us to assess and evaluate what we need to be our best selves. This may seem daunting at first, but it gets easier as you continue being mindful and learn what you need for self-care. It's like operating on a higher frequency because you know where your flaws are, and you understand where you get stuck. We put all of this together, and you get to work on being who you want to be versus being a creation of your experiences. You get to live life the way you want in an authentic way as opposed to just existing.

When does the work stop? It doesn't! You keep learning about yourself as you age. You can keep adding to your owner's manual to the point that you are an incredibly mindful person who is cool, calm, collected, and knows how to handle yourself. You get to be the best version of you. You also get to decide what that version is going to be.

Utilizing ISC allows us the freedom to live a peaceful existence. It also gives us power over what has caused us pain and suffering. We learn to operate from the standpoint of knowing ourselves and gently asking ourselves who we want to be in that moment. Intuitive self-care and mindfulness is nothing more than a gift you give yourself.

Keep track of what you are feeling and the strides you are making. Look for the positives and stay focused on how you react to things. Don't be disappointed if this doesn't come to you quickly. It took me years to figure it out, but I had to do the work to understand my mind and how it was all put together. I'm still learning about myself, but I am always aware of my balloons, and I always know what to do when they get too close.

References

APA (2018). APA Public Opinion Poll - Annual Meeting 2018. (2018, March 23-25). Retrieved from APA.com: https://www.psychiatry.org/newsroom/apa-public-opinion-poll-annual-meeting-2018

Bergland, C. (2013). The Size and Connectivity of the Amygdala Predicts Anxiety. Psychology Today.

Bremner, J. D., Elzinga, B., Schmahl, C., & Vermettan, E. (2008). Structural and Functional plasticity of the human brain in posttraumatic stress disorder. Progress in Brain Research, 171-186.

Brown, B. (2015). Daring Greatly: How the Courage to Be Vulnerable Transforms the Way We Live, Love, Parent, and Lead. New York: Penguin Random House.

Cordon, I. P. (2004). Memory for traumatic experiences in early childhood. Developmental Review, 101-132.

Davis, D. M. (2011). What Are the Benefits of Minfulness? A Practice Review of Psychotherapy-Related Research. Psychotherapy, 198-208.

Garland, S. G. (2009). The role of Mindfulness in Positive Reappraisal. Explore, 37-44.

HHP, H. M. (2018, May 1). www.health.harvard.edu. Retrieved from Understanding the stress response.

Holzel, B. K., Carmody, J., Vangel, M., Congleton, C., Yerramsetti, S., Gard, ,. T., & Lazar, S. (2011). Mindfulness practice leads to increases in regional brain gray matter density. Psychiatry Res., 36-43.

Moyer, N. M. (2019). Amygdala Hijack: When Emotion Takes Over. Retrieved from healthline.

NIMH. (n.d.). www.nimh.nih.gov. Retrieved from 5 Things you Should Know about Stress.

Sapolsky, R. P. (2019, May 2). Robert Sapolsky, Ph.D. on the Pervasive Effect of Stress: Is it killing you? Peter Attia- The Drive. (P. Attia, Interviewer)

Sisgold, S. (2013, June 4). Limited Beliefs. Retrieved from Psychology Today: https://www.psychologytoday.com/us/blog/life-in-body/201306/limitedbeliefs

Made in the USA
Monee, IL
19 February 2020

22011915R00076